Golf and the Game of Leadership

Golf and the Game of Leadership

An 18-Hole Guide for Success in Business and in Life

Donald E. McHugh

AMACOM

American Management Association

New York • Atlanta • Brussels • Chicago • Mexico City • San Francisco
Shanghai • Tokyo • Toronto • Washington, D.C.

Special discounts on bulk quantities of AMACOM books are available to corporations, professional associations, and other organizations. For details, contact Special Sales Department, AMACOM, a division of American Management Association, 1601 Broadway, New York, NY 10019.
Tel.: 212-903-8316. Fax: 212-903-8083.
Web site: www.amacombooks.org

This publication is designed to provide accurate and authoritative information in regard to the subject matter covered. It is sold with the understanding that the publisher is not engaged in rendering legal, accounting, or other professional service. If legal advice or other expert assistance is required, the services of a competent professional person should be sought.

Library of Congress Cataloging-in-Publication Data

McHugh, Donald E.
    Golf and the game of leadership : an 18-hole guide for success in business and in life / Donald E. McHugh.—1st ed.
        p.   cm.
    Includes bibliographical references and index.
    ISBN 0-8144-0837-0
    1. Leadership.   2. Success in business.   I. Title.

HD57.7.M3957   2004
658.4'092—dc22

                                                                2003022895

Printing Hole Number

10   9   8   7   6   5   4   3   2   1

*This book is dedicated to Ann.
As wife, mother, and best friend,
she is the "real leader" of the
McHugh clan and, like all the
recognized and unrecognized
"real leaders" everywhere,
makes good things happen
each and every day.*

Contents

Acknowledgments

My family has always supported me. This is a priceless gift. Ann, many times, said, "write a book based on your experiences and beliefs about leadership." Our crew—Mark and his wife Maria; Tim, Kathy, and her husband, Keith Olander; Dave, Lisa, and Kevin—echoed her request and provided significant contributions to content as well as encouragement and enthusiastic support throughout the process.

Bill Haupt, former manager of executive development at General Motors, a longtime friend and colleague, provided input, insight, and the "nitpicking" required to keep me in the fairway. He is a joy to work with, a "real leader," and a great human being. Ann and Bill participated from start to finish in making the book worthwhile, readable, and enjoyable.

Many friends and former colleagues helped along the way. My thanks to all of them, especially Chet Francke, Chuck LaSalle, Dick Lock, Mike Maggiano, Tom Olander, my brother Ray, and my nephew Mike McHugh. Fellow golfers and friends—Ken Smith, Bob Lauer, and the rest of the "Tuesday Group"—were much-appreciated cheerleaders from the first tee to the last. Christine Brennan, noted author and *sports columnist,* generously provided early writing encouragement and observations regarding the workings of the publishing industry.

Adrienne Hickey of AMACOM belongs in the text of hole #12, Courage. A self-confessed nongolfer, she nonetheless saw potential in the game of golf as a metaphor for leadership. Adrienne took a chance on a concept and a first-time author. Thanks, Adrienne. Niels Buessem did the professional editing of the manuscript. A tip of the golf cap to Niels for making the task a most enjoyable one. My thanks as well to Mike Sivilli of AMACOM for managing the overall editorial processes and book production.

And finally, special thanks to all who have contributed to my leadership, and golfing, experiences.

On the Practice Tee

On August 10, 1994 at about 3:30 in the afternoon, I was driving to Highland Meadows Golf Club in Sylvania, Ohio. Our then 20-year-old son, Kevin Michael O'Toole McHugh, was with me. Highland Meadows was not a new experience for either of us. Kevin had played there many times, including in junior golf tournaments. His sisters, Kathy and Lisa, had both worked at the Club. Kathy was the Club's office manager for several years and Lisa worked in the dining room and the office while going to college.

Kevin was home for a few days prior to beginning his junior year at the University of Michigan. He had just completed an NROTC midshipman cruise on a guided missile destroyer out of San Diego. This day he was interested in tuning up his well-above-average golfing skills. As a freshman, Kevin was invited to try out for Michigan's golf team. He missed making the team by an average of less than one stroke over five 18-hole rounds!

Kevin was enthusiastic about the opportunity to play Highland Meadows, an excellent course that annually hosts the LPGA's Jamie Farr Kroger Classic Tournament. I was along in the hope of picking up some pointers that would improve my hacker status. The conversation on the way caught me by surprise.

''Dad,'' says Kevin, ''why don't you write a book?''

''A book! About what?''

''You know, about that leadership stuff you've developed. You really know a lot from your experiences and I think you should write about them.''

''You've been talking to your mother!''

``No, really, I think you should write a book about leadership.''

Many people—family, friends, associates—can say "why
don't you" . . . and they can be easily dismissed. But when your
youngest son, last in the line of six children, says, "write a book,
Dad," eventually you just have to do it! Well, eventually is here!

So, you say, "Wait a minute, McHugh! What qualifies you to
write a book on leadership? Your son is probably biased, and
that's nice, but how about sharing some of your leadership credentials."

That's a fair request. I have been quite fortunate in that my
working career has afforded me the opportunity to serve as a
leader in a variety of organizations and at various levels of responsibility. Let me highlight my experiences.

I have held executive positions in two major *Fortune 100* corporations, General Motors Corporation (GM) and Owens-Illinois
Incorporated (O-I). During my years at GM, I pursued a program
of personal development that resulted in a master's degree from
Michigan State University and a Ph.D. from the Ohio State University. These credentials were critical to my later selection as
dean, continuing education, at the University of Toledo. And,
over a twenty-six-year military career, I've had the good fortune
to have my leadership contributions rewarded by advancement to
the rank of Captain USNR.

I believe now is the perfect time to write about leadership.
The country, the world, your loved ones, and mine, need leaders
as never before. So do our organizations. And, I submit, "real
leaders" are in short supply.

There are many books available that present theories of leadership. These are accompanied by all manner of charts utilizing
geometric shapes, matrix pigeon holes, and lots of arrows, both
linear and circular. The qualities, personalities, and styles of successful leaders, past and present, are listed. Persons of great power,
influence, or notoriety are placed under the microscope. I've decided not to go any of these routes.

"So," I say to myself, "how can I write a book about leadership that conveys what I believe are the pragmatic keys to being a successful leader? And, how can I do it in an easily understood, meaningful, helpful, and enjoyable way?" I've chosen to use the game of golf.

If you play golf, you know the spellbinding influence it has on its practitioners. For "real golfers" the game and all its subtleties and vagaries grip the soul. Golf is a marvelous blend of tests of skill and character, the quest for continuous improvement, moments of great exultation, and huge disappointment. It has its own language, rules, customs, and etiquette, which are followed religiously by those who prize the title "golfer."

If you are not a golfer, you need to make friends with one. You'll be introduced to a romantic game, which in its substance and symbolism mirrors the lessons needed for the practice of effective leadership.

The "game of golf" and the "game of leadership" metaphors should come easily to those 27 million Americans, 1.8 million Canadians, and other millions worldwide who play golf regularly. Many more millions daily attempt to play the game of leadership. Both games are played with widely, and wildly, ranging results. Success at golf is exhilarating. Failure at the game is disappointing. Success at leadership brings a sense of accomplishment. Failure at leadership can be detrimental to the leader, harmful to followers and disastrous for organizations, as illustrated, for example, by Enron, Lucent, WorldCom, Corning, LTV, Rite-Aid, and others.

This book may make you more relaxed when you go golfing, but it will not cause you to be a success on the golf course. If, however, you take its simple lessons to heart and exercise perfect practice of lessons you select, you'll be a more effective leader—what I call a "real leader"—and perhaps even a "great leader."

You probably don't determine your organization's vision, values, and strategy. However, you are expected to have the necessary technical skill and ability to manage your functional or professional area of responsibility in accordance with the established vision, values, and strategy. These are givens that will not be addressed. What I will address are the expectations of you as a leader of people, that is, how do you combine the efforts of others so that your organization thrives and survives.

I facilitate a leadership development program for technical people. The participants are mostly engineers. At the beginning of the first day of the program, I ask, "Are there any engineers in the room?" As you probably expect, most of the people raise their hands. And, I say, "You must be in the wrong room, this is a program for leaders."

No, I've never been thrown out of the room. The point is made! Leadership is a different game. There is a difference between being an engineer with leadership concerns and being a leader with an engineering background. We move on from there.

So, I ask that you see yourself as a person with technical or professional skills and experiences that are not to be discarded. They are important to you and your understanding of what needs to be accomplished. But the job now is "the leadership of others" in the context of the organization's vision, values, and strategy. Therefore, my focus throughout this book is on you. We'll look at the attitudes, behaviors, and actions your followers, and others, expect from you as leader.

Golf and leadership rest on similar foundations of fundamental concepts. Both are games for the individual. The golfer must hit his or her own ball. The leader must decide the next move. Consequently, each must accept the responsibility for the results.

This book is meant for you, the leadership tournament player, the organizational leader on the front line working to make things happen. It is you who must do the right things, in the right way, if goals are to be achieved. You've probably not been anointed, didn't marry the chairman's son or daughter, and weren't born with a silver putter in your hand! You are simply a hard-working person, with sleeves rolled up, dedicated to being the best leader you can be, and beyond that let the putts drop where they may.

Though the "top of the organization hitters" are not the primary focus for this book, I do invite them to join us as we play the round. After all, you need their support and example if you are to be the very best leader you can be. They should be aware of what we are talking about.

In writing about Inspector Thomas Lynley, principal character in her mystery novel *For the Sake of Elena*, Elizabeth George muses: "Having not read university writing in years, Lynley smiled in amusement. He'd forgotten that tendency of the academician to voice his pronouncements with such egregious pomposity." Many have written thoughtfully about leadership. In like manner, others have written about it in academic fashion. I intend these pages to be thoughtful and wise but above all pragmatically useful to you in your pursuit of leadership effectiveness.

Whether leadership can or cannot be taught, it most certainly can be learned. We can all be our own best teachers. Honest self-evaluation, plus a little help from those around us who wish our success, can give us a good handle on our capabilities. When we teach ourselves, we have the unique opportunity to sort through and apply the wisdom of generations. We can all learn from the great leaders of the past and present, just as the golfer attempts to learn from the golfing greats. But, we must know what to look for and how to apply it. This includes learning what not to do, which may be the best lesson of all!

The round you are about to play is one I've played for many years with some measurable success. As a golfer, though I love the game, I am not, nor have I ever been, anything close to a "scratch player." However, I have long felt the confidence of a low handicap leader.

Over the years I've had to adapt my leadership skills to meet change, just as the golfer must adapt to play a hole, a course, and the elements. I've played a lot of leadership rounds. I've observed many other leaders play their rounds as well. I try to help others to be more effective leaders through facilitated leadership development activities. It is the wisdom gained through these efforts I wish to share with you. My approach is to bring together the challenges of leadership and the challenges of the game Kevin and I went out to play on that August day in 1994, the marvelous game of golf. It is a lifelong addiction for many, and the numbers keep increasing. Golf is a near perfect metaphor for leadership.

The game of golf and the game of leadership both offer challenge. Each presents obstacles to success. Excellent performance in each game is rewarded. New challenges in each game are just over the horizon. Golf and leadership, to be played well, require understanding and consistent practice of basic fundamentals. Both demand, for most of us, the necessity of practice. Tools are available for each game, and in each, tool selection is up to the player. Both are games for the thinking person. Both require the use of management skill. You cannot consistently win at either game if you are not positive and optimistic about the results of your play. Possibly above all, the game of golf and the game of leadership require total focus and concentration if optimum results are to be achieved. We will illustrate further as we play the leadership course.

The game of golf is a test of the individual. So is the game of leadership. Success at golf or leadership rests on the application of fundamental skills refined through practice, performance, and repetition. Master the skills required to play golf and you can consistently shoot respectable scores at any age. Master the skills of playing the leadership game and you can be an effective leader over time.

My hope for the following pages is that they provide you with reinforcement of your individual leadership skills and thoughtful opportunities for increasing your leadership effectiveness. You know, move your leadership scores from above 100 to the 90s, from the 90s to the 80s, and from the 80s to the 70s. If you legitimately find yourself consistently leading in the 70s, let me know how you do it for my next book!

A full golf course consists of 18 holes of play. These holes vary in length and difficulty. Each hole is assigned a "par," the number of golf shots expected of a good golfer to complete the hole. Par can be 3, 4, or 5, based principally on the length of the hole. The total of par for the 18 holes is most often 72 but can be 70, 71, or even 73, depending on the course layout. Using our golf metaphor for leadership, we have named our chapters "holes."

The first six holes of the Global Leadership Course are straightforward requirements for a successful player of the leadership game. A leader should par these holes as a foundation for moving on to hole #7, "The Slight Edge," which discusses the need to increase leadership effectiveness. Holes #8 through #18 provide insight into how you as a leader can develop a slight edge in your leadership skills.

Enjoy the round!

THE
GLOBAL
LEADERSHIP
COURSE

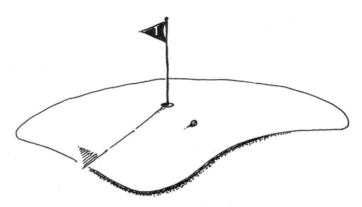

You've Gotta Love the Game

The question is: Which comes first, enjoying the game or playing it well? I believe the golfer who drives into the parking lot anticipating a good time can't help but play well most of the time. There's something to be said for optimism and a carefree spirit.[1]

Corey Pavin, 1995 U.S. Open champion

The object of this book is not to offer false hope or promise of an instant cure for every leadership ill you have experienced or may experience in the future. No long-hidden secrets will be revealed. In truth, the only secret to playing a better leadership game is that there is "no secret at all." There is no shortcut to improvement just as there are no shortcuts to playing a better game of golf. If you want to become a more effective leader, take to heart and practice the advice and wisdom contained in these pages. It will help. But, if you really want to excel, you will really believe it in your heart and gut. You will fall in love with the game! You will seek to play the leadership game with the dedication of the avid golfers portrayed in the following examples.

> A television commercial played over and over again a few years ago showed a golfer sitting on a bench in a small three-sided shelter covered by a roof. He is alone with his golf clubs. It is raining. No, it is pouring! He continues to wait. Another golfer arrives. They agree to partner-up. They optimistically observe, ``it's letting up some.'' The downpour continues. They sit on the bench. Waiting.
>
> Roger Maltbie, the TV golf commentator and former PGA professional, did a television special about the bands of golfers—especially those in large metropolitan areas—who vie for weekend tee times at public courses. This includes waiting for the opening of morning registration by literally spending the night in line. Pity them and their perseverance when they suffer the fate of the golfers in the television commercial.
>
> On balmy weekday afternoons during spring, summer, and fall, people across the country who are supposed to be working show up for a round of 18. Sunday church attendance drops with the advent of good golfing weather.

What brings these people out? What causes them to so want to play the game of golf? In a word, MOTIVATION! Golfers are motivated by the game they love to play, the game that never ceases to challenge. There are millions of us. And the numbers keep growing.

Love It Too Much?

In November of 1862, the Union Army of the Potomac under General Burnside was preparing to cross the Rappahannock River, capture Fredericksburg, and move on to Richmond. Burnside was delayed several days awaiting delivery of the pontoon bridges needed to cross the river. The delay allowed General Robert E. Lee to bring in reinforcements and to set up a defense on the south side of the river, where Lee felt he could contain the superior Union forces.

When Burnside began his assault, it was too late. Lee's defenses worked perfectly. The Union army was badly defeated, and Burnside's surviving forces retreated to Washington. After the battle, Lee and his staff inspected the considerable damage done to Fredericksburg. Upon seeing the ruins, Lee observed to his staff, "It is good that war is so horrible. If it were not we should grow to love it too much!"

Motivation or Movement

You and I have observed people succeed and fail in the organizational workplace. Success or failure, given the ability to perform, rests on more than going through the motions to reach a goal or earn a paycheck. What is it that motivates people, most importantly leaders, to perform to the best of their ability. What causes them to love what they do?

One of the questions most frequently asked by aspiring leaders is "how do I motivate my people?" First, we need to understand that people follow leaders either because they are internally or externally moved to do so. Figure 1-1 illustrates this distinction. We can pull or push people to do what needs to be done. Both can be hard work. Both can be unsuccessful. Ideally they will want to do it, that is, they are internally motivated.

Many leaders believe they have people skills and that they can use them to motivate others. They cannot! What they can do is attempt to establish a motivational environment that will, we hope, influence the desired behavior. Individuals control their own motivation. You do, so do I. Sure, golfers can be pulled, or pushed, into waiting for the rain to stop, or waiting in line before dawn for a tee time, or skipping work to play golf, but they've got

FIGURE 1-1.
External movement and internal motivation.

1. People can be pulled in a direction.

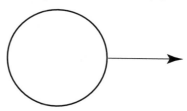

2. People can be pushed in a direction.

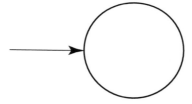

3. People respond to internal motivation.

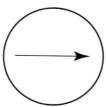

to want to do it to enjoy it and do their very best. They respond to an internal motivation, so do your followers.

Herzberg's Theory

Dr. Frederick Herzberg, who developed a classic theory of motivation in the workplace, is remembered as one of the most influential management teachers of our time. In 1995, Herzberg's book, *Work and the Nature of Man*, was listed as "one of the ten most important books impacting management theory and practice in the twentieth century." His 1968 *Harvard Business Review* article, *One More Time: How Do You Motivate Employees*, most recently reissued in January 2003, is the all-time best-selling *HBR* reprint by thousands of copies.

I had the pleasure of meeting Fred Herzberg and introducing him to a group of several hundred General Motors leaders in Dayton, Ohio. I am convinced he was not thinking about the game of golf as he developed his theory of motivation in the workplace. But I am equally certain that he was thinking about how to generate in the organizational workplace the zeal represented by an enthusiastic golfer. In my opinion, Herzberg's theory stands to this day as the most practical, realistic, logical, common-sense yet academically sound, analysis of the subject.

Herzberg's theory states that an individual's motivation is influenced by "hygiene" and "motivation" factors. The *hygiene factors* in an organization—also referred to as *maintenance factors*—are such things as company policy and administration, leadership and supervision, working conditions, salary, and job security.

People expect hygiene factors to be appropriately provided. Hygiene factors possess little potential for motivation. They are expected. If they are not provided, people will be unhappy and dissatisfied. Provide them and people will not be happy and satisfied. They will simply not be unhappy and not dissatisfied.

Motivation Factors

Herzberg's motivation factors involve what we ask people to do and include the following:

- Achievement
- Recognition
- Responsibility
- Growth
- Challenging Work

These factors, together with acceptable hygiene factors, can result in satisfaction on the job. Achievement and recognition are short-term motivators and need repetition. Awards, promotions, and merit salary increases are good examples. We appreciate them but quickly revert to "what have you done for me lately." Responsibility, growth, and challenging work are longer lasting. Interestingly, motivated people do not necessarily experience all of the motivational factors. Some can be motivated by the work they do but not experience growth or added responsibility. Although their efforts may not be recognized, they are satisfied with their own measurement of their achievements. For example, many golfers are motivated simply by the challenge and the joy of playing the game.

When the motivation factors are not being met, people will stress the hygiene or maintenance factors. When motivation factors are met, people tend to view hygiene factors as being less important. The most powerful motivational factor is challenging work. If we look, for example, at the auto industry, it is easy to understand the lack of motivational opportunity offered an assembly line worker. Hence, in that industry people stress maintenance factors. If leaders provide only the hygiene factors they can expect minimal effort, mediocre performance, and in a highly competitive world, results that don't "make the cut." Provide the maintenance factors together with the motivation factors and you will increase your chances of getting spirited effort, extraordinary performance, and results that put you and your team on "the leader board." Figure 1-2 is an illustration of the Herzberg theory applied to our golfing metaphor.

The impact of Herzberg's theory on the leader intent on creating and sustaining a motivational organization environment is clear. Southwest Airlines, one of the most successful U.S. airlines of the past fifteen years, appears to put life in Herzberg's theory. Joan Magretta, in her book, *What Management Is: How It Works and Why It's Everyone's Business*, comments that under the leadership of President Herb Kelleher, Southwest's culture has been responsible for keeping employees happy, satisfied, dedicated, and energetic. The idea that work should be fun is one of Southwest's core values. The company also adheres to the notion that every

FIGURE 1-2.
The Herzberg theory.

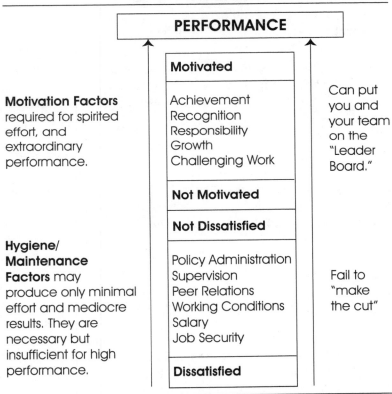

person makes a difference and everyone should be treated with dignity and respect.

Love It! You'll Enjoy It!

How many golfers do you know who do not love the game? How many will, whenever there is the opportunity, voluntarily head to the golf course? How many are dissatisfied or unhappy when they are "forced" to play the game? How many professional golfers are not motivated by the game itself? You know the answers to these questions. Golfers see all the motivation factors in the game and respond accordingly. They not only love the "work," they have fun playing the game. Well, most of the time!

The game of leadership has the same potential for motivation as the game of golf. Where is there greater opportunity to experience the motivation factors than as a leader in the organizational context? Leaders, like golfers, never run out of challenges. Leadership offers the "real leader" the internal satisfaction only it can bring: To know that you have helped others to succeed. Leaders need to provide these same motivational opportunities to their followers.

Leadership is personal. It does not come from corporate headquarters. An honest, heartfelt interest in serving people is more important than perfectly polished skills. Leaders know their people. They give their heart to them. When you really care, it shows through. You can't fake being a "people person."

Charlie

Doing nice things for his workers was a trademark of Charles Butcher's leadership. Butcher took over the family's Massachusetts-based cleaning-products business from his father and uncle in the mid-1950s. In September 2000, Butcher—known as "Charlie" among his employees—told the Worcester, Massachusetts *Telegram & Gazette*, "I believe the only way to treat people is to have them happy at all times. They do twice the amount of work when they are happy."

Charlie Butcher understood that his company's success was due in large part to the people he employed. He demonstrated over many years his concern for the well-being of the men and women on the shop floor. Paul McLaughlin, president of the Butcher Company, summed up Charlie's feelings about his employees in this quote from the *Telegram & Gazette*: "Charlie Butcher is one of those rare men who really likes people. He loved to see the cars in the parking lot because he knew people were at work."[2]

I think Fred Herzberg would have loved Charlie Butcher.

We'll tell you more about Charlie when we get to hole #13. Now, if you can't wait, go there for "the rest of the story."

If you love golf, you've got to love leadership. And if you're not a golfer, if you are a motivated person and accept the metaphor, you should love it as well. We'll show you in the following chapters how to score well and have fun as you play the leadership game. Golfers who do not score reasonably well—and more importantly, who don't have fun playing the game, for whatever reason—usually stop playing golf. Leaders who do not lead effectively and/or do not enjoy the game of leadership should find other avenues to pursue, both for their own well-being and for that of those they are responsible for leading.

Golfers must work hard to be successful, and in the end they must do it themselves. Leaders also have to work hard to be successful, and how they do it is up to them. Substitute the word leadership for golf in the following quote and measure your leadership effectiveness as we continue our round.

Let your attitude determine your golf game.
Don't let your golf game determine your attitude.[3]
Davis Love, Jr., 1997 PGA champion

Quick Tips for Improving Your Leadership Game

Real leaders typically understand and model the following in their day-to-day actions.

- Lead with passion!
- Love the challenges!
- Celebrate the successes!

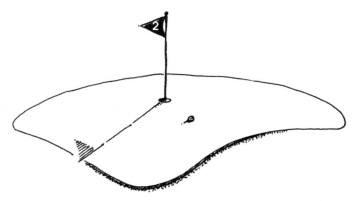

Simple . . . yet Difficult

If I keep things simple, I play better.

Nancy Lopez, member of the LPGA Hall of Fame
and the World Golf Hall of Fame

Golf is a simple game. There are a series of 18 small holes, filled
with cups, spread over an appealing, well-tended landscape. These
holes (cups) are placed at intervals of roughly 100 to 500 yards on
beautifully manicured grassy surfaces (greens). The object of the
game is to move a small white (usually) ball (golf ball) from hole
to hole in a programmed sequence (front, or first nine, then back,
or second nine) until the player has struck the golf ball into each
of the 18 holes. This task is accomplished by using the tools of the
game, appropriately called golf clubs, which come in various
lengths and angled striking surfaces. The player (golfer) simply
takes a club of choice and strikes the golf ball in the direction of
the appropriate hole as often as necessary until it nestles safely in
the cup on the green. Then on to the next hole, all the while

counting the number of times a club is used to advance the ball. The total number of club swings is tallied for each hole from hole 1 through hole 18. The total for all 18 holes is the golfer's game (round) score.

As you know, or can imagine, some golfers use their clubs more often than others to accomplish the objective of putting the golf ball in each of the 18 holes. Golfers compare their total number of swings (missing the ball also counts as a swing) with the totals of other players to determine who did the best, i.e., who had the lowest number of club swings. In addition, the people who developed the golfing landscape (course) tell you how many swings you should have taken on each hole. This varies from three to five swings per hole and usually totals 70 to 72 for the 18 holes. The golfer plays against these benchmarks, which are referred to as "par."

Many books about leadership attempt to teach or train people to be leaders. My intention is to help you in your efforts to learn how to lead more effectively. I'll not attempt to teach you the game of golf or how to play it. However, if you are new to the game of golf, you will have the opportunity to learn about the game. Hopefully, I'll pique your interest in giving it a try. As we play the Global Leadership Course, I'll provide some specifics about the game of golf. And a glossary of golf terms is available in the Pro Shop at the end of the book.

A Little Golf Folklore

You may be curious as to why full-length golf courses have 18 holes, and not ten, or a dozen, or twenty, or more. Do you know the reason?

Golfers know that Scotland is generally acclaimed as the birthplace of golf, and certainly of the game as we play it today. Legend has it that during a discussion among the club's membership board at St. Andrews in 1858, one of the members pointed out that it took exactly 18 shots to polish off a fifth of Scotch. By limiting himself to only one shot of Scotch per hole, the Scot figured that a round of golf was finished when the Scotch ran out. Hence, 18 holes. Fact or fiction, I like the story!

A Tough Course

The model for the Global Leadership Course discussed in this book is the Black Course of the historic Inverness Club in Toledo, Ohio. Inverness was originally designed by the late Scottish-born architect, Donald Ross. It is recognized as one of America's great golf courses. Most of the golfing greats have strolled the fairways of Inverness during its long history. It has been selected as the site for the 1920, 1931, 1957, and 1979 USGA Open Championships, the 1973 USGA Amateur Championship, the 1986 and 1993 PGA Championships, and the 2003 USGA Senior Open Championship. At first glance, Inverness appears to be a simple golfing layout. But ask a club member or any of the professionals and top amateurs who have played the course and they will tell you that Inverness is a very difficult course. Long par-4s, narrow fairways, and small, fast, undulating greens create a true golfing challenge. Inverness is a difficult golf course to play but a prestigious one. It is an appropriate model for the Global Leadership Course, which is also more difficult to play than it first appears but when played well rewards the leader who wishes to achieve the status of a "real leader."

Low scores in the game of golf most often result when players do a good job at three aspects of the game. They are:

1. Keeping the "ball in the fairway"
2. Hitting "greens in regulation" (which means using no more than two shots on a par 4 and three shots on a par 5 hole)
3. Having a good "short game" (which is pitching and putting)

These essentials, especially her outstanding short game, led to the unlikely victory of twenty-four-year-old Hilary Lunke in the

2003 U. S. Women's Open. The 6,550 yard Pumpkin Ridge Witch Hollow course in North Plains, Oregon, site of the Open, was the longest course in U.S. Women's Open history. Lunke, whose driving distance average is one of the shortest on the LPGA Tour had difficulty hitting greens in regulation due to the course length but did well keeping the ball in the fairway and won with masterful pitching and putting. In the three-way playoff for the championship, Lunke took only 23 putts for the 18 holes. She told the Associated Press, "I did not have 100 percent of my ball-striking. But I had 150 percent of my putting." Such extraordinary performance in one aspect of the game led to Lunke's victory. However, her success over time, and that of any other golfer, rests on consistent performance in all aspects of the game.

Leadership is also a simple game. Its essence, like that of golf, is skilled execution of key fundamentals. Management guru Peter F. Drucker says common sense is the foundation of leadership. But common sense is not so common. Leaders too often seem to work very hard at making the game of leadership unnecessarily difficult. Drucker further points out that, not unlike golf, leadership is centered on the integration of three central ingredients, "contribution to the mission of the organization, concentration on key tasks, and commitment to professional standards of performance."

Golf and the Game of Leadership is about hitting quality shots in the leadership game from wherever your responsibility lies. It is about helping you to stay in the leadership fairway. Just as the golfer concentrates on achieving the right results with each swing of a golf club, so too the leader's energy must be concentrated on accomplishing the right results.

Challenge at General Motors

Maryann Keller, in her book *Rude Awakening: The Rise, Fall and Struggle for Recovery of General Motors*, wrote, "What kind of place is [General Motors] really? . . . It might surprise you to learn it's the kind of place great novels are made of, full of drama, intrigue, and high adventure. What goes on here may well be the ultimate example of the heartbeat of American business. GM is a study in many of the things that are right about corporate America . . . and much that is wrong."[1]

In the mid-to-late 1980s, GM, faced with increasing competition and technological challenges, was going through major change in every aspect of its business. The corporation was building new plants, revamping old ones, introducing robotics, retraining the workforce, trying a new method of operating (in Saturn), and reorganizing on a massive scale. In one organizational realignment more than 200,000 employees changed organizational identities in a single day.

A McKinsey and Company study, commissioned by GM, confirmed that the systemic changes were essential but found other aspects of the business that needed attention. Specifically, the organization's leadership culture needed to change. It was as if GM was building new golf courses, revamping old ones, requiring the use of new golf equipment, training the caddies and grounds crews, and reorganizing their country clubs. All at the same time. But, they were not helping the leadership adapt to the changes affecting their game.

Task forces were assembled to set specific goals for implementing McKinsey's recommendations. One task force looked at the matter of executive development. A resulting objective was to develop a core GM-specific leadership development program for the top 500 executives. This assignment fell to the corporation's manager of executive development, Bill Haupt. GM's education and training department (GME&T) was technically competent to build the program, but it recognized the need to have a credible outside partner. They chose the Forum Corporation, based in Boston.

In the two-week period just before Christmas 1985, Dr. William M. DeMarco, Forum's senior project consultant, and Bill Haupt traveled the country interviewing a diagonal slice of forty-five upper-level GM executives. Three basic questions were at the heart of the interviews:

- What words would you use to describe GM today?
- How would you like to be able to describe GM as we enter the twenty-first century?
- What is getting in the way?

Simple Answers

The answers were remarkable. Remarkably simple! Every person asked—man or woman—said in response to the last question, "We are." Surprisingly, they did not blame unfair trade with Japan, government regulations, the attitudes of the workforce, the union(s), or provide any other lame excuse. They were leaders. They knew that to get different results they had to lead differently. They knew the answer was leadership. That was simple. They also admitted they did not know quite how to change. That was difficult.

GME&T and Forum then developed a "culture change" training course for GM's top 3,000 managers. The effort was originally entitled "Leadership 21." But the pilot group, demonstrating an uncommon sense of urgency, seized ownership and demanded the program be called "Leadership NOW." Then in a move I greatly appreciated, Bill Haupt and his boss, Ralph Frederick, director of GME&T, invited me to partner with Forum's lead facilitator, Marc Sarkady, in the conduct of the program.

We ran the first pilot in late 1986. Then we ran 102 groups in the United States, plus twelve groups in Europe. We finished in 1990. As I recall, the total number of participants was between 2,900 and 3,000. Participants came from all functional areas and all parts of the GM system.

I estimate that more than thirty corporate officers and other top-level executives served as evening discussion leaders. Many follow-up Walk-the-Talk workshops were also conducted.

What is remarkable is that the GM program administrators never had top level permission to do any of it! They got an okay to run a pilot and just never stopped. Their bosses just let them do it. It is indeed easier to get forgiveness than permission.

A Course Change

Did "Leadership NOW" by itself change GM's culture? Of course not! But did it contribute to the push for needed culture change? Absolutely! General Motors is like one of our modern giant cruise ships. If you want to change the course of one of these vessels, the officer-of-the-deck orders a change to the angle of the rudder. The rudder angle changes the course degree by degree, and it is readjusted from time to time until the new course is reached. "Leadership NOW" was a one-degree change in the movement of GM to a new course, a new culture. It gave impetus to the many changes that have followed since.

According to Maryann Keller:

> Executives who attended the sessions experienced initial culture shock as they were asked to drop their inhibitions and relate to one another with complete trust . . . anonymous employee evaluations were discussed openly in sessions . . . words like "open" and "honest" were used frequently. It was a very different experience for the people at General Motors—part sensitivity training, part personal empowerment. The tone of the sessions threw people off guard—they were the epitome of everything GM had never been.[2]

Since the time of Leadership NOW, GM has made significant strides in its culture and products. So has their competition. And the struggle continues. One thing appears evident, GM is trying to eliminate, or reduce, unnecessary internal actions that increase the difficulty of the task. The corporation is searching for simplicity of operation as it competes in the global car and truck marketplace.

The approach of Jack Smith and Rick Wagoner as leaders of GM has greatly simplified GM's business approach. The emphasis is back to engineering, building, and selling "great cars and trucks." The "frozen middle," a term coined by former GM Chairman Roger Smith to describe an unmotivated middle-management group created in no small part by the actions of top management, appears to be thawing. The reason is a leadership that is working hard on implementing its twenty-first-century vision, values, and strategy from the top to the bottom of the organization.

Are You a Good Golfer?

It was a beautiful morning. The golfer set up his ball on the first tee (the starting position for each hole), took a mighty swing, and hit his ball into a clump of trees. He found the ball and saw an opening between two trees through which he thought he could hit it. Taking a club from his bag, he took another mighty swing. The ball hit a tree, bounced back, hit him in the forehead and killed him. As he approached the Gates of Heaven, St. Peter saw him coming and asked, "Are you a good golfer?" To which the man replied, "Got here in two, didn't I!"

There are an estimated 27 million golfers in the United States. They play the game with varying degrees of success. In fact, though the game of golf, as just described, is quite simple and straightforward, it is reported that only about 10 percent of golfers score less than 100 strokes for 18 holes played—a surprisingly low percentage considering that golf is such a "simple game."

As Bill Laimbeer, former NBA star with the Detroit Pistons and an excellent golfer, told Paul W. Smith on Smith's WJR Detroit morning radio show on October 29, 1997, "the ball doesn't move and nobody's guarding it!"[3] Yet, two months earlier on the then ABC-TV *Regis and Kathy Lee Show*, Troy Aikman, former star quarterback for the Dallas Cowboys and also a good amateur golfer, said that golf "is a game nobody can master. . . . You come off the course and always feel you could have done better."[4]

Playing a complete round of golf requires a minimum of 18 shots. Such a round, it is safe to say, is impossible despite the marvelous skills exhibited by the likes of Tiger Woods, Phil Mickelson, Annika Sorenstam, Julie Inkster, Ernie Els, Laura Davies, Sergio Garcia, and Karrie Webb. The very best competitive rounds recorded have been in the high 50s, and there have been very few. Absolute perfection is impossible in golf. It is also impossible in organizational life, as the challenges to the giant GM indicate. So, too, it is impossible to be a perfect leader. However, just as the golfer continually strives for perfection and the organization strives for positive survival, so too the real leader strives to be the best he or she can be.

The game of golf and the game of leadership are both simple, yet difficult. Both have rules for play and codes of conduct. Players in each game succeed or fail in relationship to goals and objectives. Each game requires focus, practice, adherence to fundamentals, mental and physical stability, and an array of personal qualities, abilities, attitudes and behaviors that are amazingly similar. Both games are built on foundations of solid values. Let's examine the values that support golf and leadership as we continue our round.

Odds on scoring a hole-in-one are 1 in 42,000.

Paul Harvey, radio commentator

Quick Tips for Improving Your Leadership Game

Real leaders typically understand and model the following in their day-to-day actions:

■ LEAD BY EXAMPLE: Simple, yet difficult

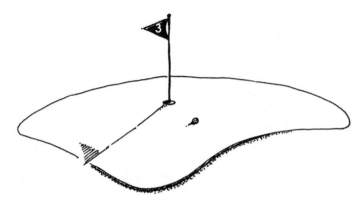

Values Are the Drivers

Golf is a game based on honor, not on trying to get away with something.

Jim Nance, CBS-TV golf commentator,
2001 Memorial tournament

This hole is about the concept of values, namely the attitudes and beliefs that drive our behaviors. These values are drawn from our life experiences and brought to the life we live. Many are manifested in our approach to both the game of golf and the game of leadership. Our core values guide our actions. The values of integrity and honesty are crucial determinants of the degree of trust people place in us as leaders. Comments regarding values are sprinkled throughout this book, we cannot escape them. They come into play on every hole.

To value is to highly respect, to prize, and to appreciate. The game of golf and the game of leadership are value based. As a leader, it is important to know what your people value. Their values will guide them in following you and in helping to achieve organizational goals. And they will know your values because you will make them known by your actions.

The Core of Character

Values are at the core of character. They help us determine the rightness of our actions. They are not made on the golf course or in the leadership setting but they are revealed in these environments. Many of the values required to be a "real golfer" are the values required to be a "real leader." Both focus on doing what is right and valuing the opportunity to do so. It is interesting to note that golf's values have been time-tested. They have maintained their integrity. Is this true of your experience with the expression of leadership values?

Leadership Values

The CEO of a major company was visited by the CEO of another large, noncompeting organization from a different industry. The visitor's purpose was to learn how the host company managed the performance evaluations of its leaders. The host company CEO was recognized internationally for his ability to develop leaders. There were always sufficient numbers of qualified candidates for promotional openings. The company was also a fertile source of candidates for executive positions at other companies.

The host CEO drew the diagram shown in Figure 3-1 on a piece of note paper, handed it to his visitor, and explained how his company evaluates its leaders: "We objectively look at our leaders in terms of their placement in one of the four quadrants of this diagram. They are rated Low to High on results achieved and in terms of adherence to company values.

1. High Results and High Values: the person is recognized and rewarded.
2. Low Results and High Values: the person is coached to bring the results up.
3. Low Results and Low Values: the person is let go.

FIGURE 3-1.
Results + Values = Recognition + Reward.

	LOW — RESULTS — HIGH	
HIGH V A L U E S LOW	COACH	RECOGNIZE AND REWARD
	LET GO	COACH COUNSEL LET GO

HIGH

	COACH	RECOGNIZE
V		AND
A		REWARD
L		
U		
E	LET GO	COACH
S		COUNSEL
		LET GO

LOW   RESULTS   HIGH

4. High Results and Low Values: the person is coached and counseled. If the values results do not improve the person is let go."

The clear message to the visiting CEO was that adherence to company values was required of leadership—not just good results. In fact, good results without adherence to values was considered unacceptable. The same is true in golf. A score that is illicitly or incorrectly obtained is unacceptable and can be disqualifying. You're out of the competition!

Calling a Penalty

Rules govern each of the various sports played in the United States, and in most cases they apply on a worldwide basis. They form the fabric for fair play and in most sports are difficult to change because they protect the values of the sport. The rules are enforced by referees, umpires, and other officials. However, some players seem to stretch the rules whenever they can. This is especially true in football and basketball. The most egregious violation is the common practice of "holding" one's opponent, both on the football field and on the basketball court. It is often called by officials, and penalties are assessed.

It also seems that "holding" is often overlooked. When that happens, does the football or basketball player who holds an opponent in violation of the rules request a timeout to notify the officials that a penalty should have been called? NO WAY! Football and basketball players do not stand in line to report their violations of the rules. Do you think they should?

In contrast to those sports in which players sometimes appear to be trying to get away with as much as they can, the game of golf expects you to call penalties on yourself. As an example, Tom Lehman, a professional since 1982, did just that in the 1997 British Open. He called a two-shot penalty on himself for playing his ball from the wrong place.

Also, Meg Mallon, playing in the first round of the 1996 LPGA Jamie Farr Kroger Classic, led the field with a 6-under-par 65. During her round, on the 17th green, she had a 15-foot putt die (stop) on the lip of the cup. She thought the ball was still moving and so she waited, anticipating it would drop in. It did. However, in waiting 18 seconds for the ball to drop, because she thought it was moving, she applied the wrong rule. The ball overhung the lip of the cup and therefore was subject to the 10 seconds allowed by rule, without unreasonable delay, to see if the ball would drop. She took a score of 4 on the par-5 hole, finished her round, and signed and turned in her scorecard. She should have taken a penalty stroke for exceeding the 10-second limitation.

Following evening conversations with some of her fellow pros, and a sleepless night, she advised LPGA officials of her concern that she may have turned in an incorrect scorecard. TV tapes were reviewed and they verified her mistake. Meg Mallon was disqualified for having signed an incorrect scorecard, the first disqualification of a tournament leader in LPGA history.

Other professionals have reported and been penalized for their violations of the rules of golf. It is not uncommon. If you were playing in a local tournament and encountered circumstances similar to either Lehman's or Mallon's, would you report it and take the penalty?

Making the Tough Call

A high school golf team in the East wins the state tournament title. On the way home from the matches, the team's coach reviews the scorecards. He finds a two-stroke error, which increases his team's score. He reports the error and returns the championship trophy. The team is disqualified for having turned in the wrong score. What will the coach and team take away from this disappointing experience? As a leader, in a comparable business situation, what would you do? What have you done?

Would You Hire This Man?

A young marine stationed at Quantico, Virginia is advised that a man identified as his elderly father is the victim of a hit-and-run accident. The marine is granted emergency leave and arrives at an Atlanta hospital shortly after midnight. The duty nurse briefs him on the condition of his father, who probably does not have long to live. The young man enters the hospital room. He sees the old man in his bed surrounded by life support equipment. The young man hesitates for a moment and then he pulls a chair over to the side of the bed. He sits down, takes the old man's hand and begins talking to him. Every once in a while he feels what could be a tug of recognition from the hand he is holding.

Shortly after 5 A.M., the old man passes away. The marine ends his bedside vigil and advises the nurse of the old man's death. And then he asks, "Who was that old man?"

The nurse is stunned, "Why, he's your father."

"No, he's not," says the young man. "I never saw him before tonight."

"I don't understand, why didn't you say so earlier?"

"Well, it was clear he wouldn't last long. I thought if he felt I was his son it would help him to go peacefully."

The nurse, clearly impressed, said, "That's so thoughtful. People just don't show that much caring for others. Why would you do it?"

The marine replied without hesitation, "I was just doing what my mother taught me. She told me that when I grew up I would be faced with many situations not of my making. Sometimes, I would be in the position of being in the right place at the wrong time. At other times, I would be in the wrong place at the right time. The measure of me, she said, will be how I handle those situations."

Do you have some understanding of the values of the young marine? Would he be able to accept and pursue the values of your organization? Would you hire him based on what you know of his values?

Father Knows Best

All golf fans know of Phil Mickleson's perennial quest for a victory in a "major" tournament. Phil, at this writing, is a twenty-time winner on the PGA tour. But he has not won in forty-two attempts to capture a "major" title, namely the Masters, the U.S. Open, the British Open, or the PGA Championship. Some were undoubtedly surprised when he did not play for several weeks leading up to the 2003 Masters. The Augusta course is well suited to Phil's game strengths and many felt that it would offer him the best chance to win his first major. He had even skipped play in the Ford Motor Company-sponsored tournament at Doral, which was unusual because Phil is Ford's featured PGA personality in its television advertising.

Why did Mickleson limit his activity prior to the Masters? Was he injured? Was he working privately to improve his game? No, he went home to be with his wife as she awaited the birth of their third child! Johnny Miller, the master of candor in golf commentary, was quoted in *USA Today* regarding Mickleson's behavior, "Maybe he's a better father than a lot of pros in the past. [I know] my career came way second."[1] What would you have done? I say, way to go Phil, Johnny, and Ford!

Walk-the-Talk

The often-used value phrase "walk-the-talk" poses the need for leadership to match its organizational policies, pronouncements, and actions. In a recent conversation with a strategy planner for a major corporation, I was advised of an equal opportunity problem perceived by the planner.

"Our top management is too young! This hurts us now, and will increasingly do so in the future. Already we are experiencing a poor use of older people and a reduction in their morale and motivation. A fixation on youth has caused us to devalue the experience and dedication of our longer service employees. There is little opportunity for people 45 to 50 and older now, and down the road there will be decreased opportunity for young people. We've created an imbalance in our human resource structure that threatens future success. The environment in the organization, as represented by our practices, doesn't match up with our proclaimed equal career development policy." As a leader, what value do you place on age and experience? Does your organization walk-the-talk regarding its human resource policies and practices?

Noel M. Tichy, author of *The* Leadership *Engine*, comments on the power of values:

> Winning leaders have turned to emphasizing values for purely practical reasons. . . . A typical GE manager [supervises] fifteen to twenty and sometimes more [subordinates]. The point is simple: When you can't control, dictate, or monitor, the only thing you can do is trust. And that means leaders have to be sure that the people they are trusting have values that are going to elicit the decisions and actions they want.[2]

Organizational Values

Organizations, large and small, have increasingly recognized the need for, and the power of, values. Successful organizations, those that sustain themselves over time, are guided by clearly stated core values that leaders are expected to model and uphold.

General Electric, a company that has survived the nineteenth and twentieth centuries and continues its excellent performance in the twenty-first century, holds the following values:

GE Values
Driving a 21st-Century GE
Respecting Always the Three Traditions of GE:
Unyielding Integrity, Commitment to Performance, and
Thirst for Change

- *Passion for Our Customers*: Measuring our success by that of our customers . . . always driven by Six Sigma quality and a spirit of innovation
- *Meritocracy*: Creating opportunities for the best people from around the world to grow and live their dreams
- *Growth Driven, Globally Oriented*: Growing our people, markets and businesses around the world
- *Every Person, Every Idea Counts*: Respecting the individual and valuing contributions of each employee
- *Playing Offense*: Using the advantages of size to take risks and try new things . . . never allowing size to be a disadvantage
- *Embracing Speed and Excellence*: Using the benefits of a digital age to accelerate our success and build a faster and smarter GE
- *Living the Hallmarks of GE Leadership*:
    - Passion for learning and sharing ideas
    - Committed to delivering results in every environment
    - Ability to energize and inspire global, diverse teams
    - Connected to workplace, customers and communities . . . in touch with the world"[3]

Similarly, General Motors Corporation has an established set of core values.

- *Customer Enthusiasm:* We will dedicate ourselves to products and services that create enthusiastic customers. No one will be second-guessed for doing the right thing for the customer.
- *Continuous Improvement:* We will set ambitious goals, stretch to meet them, and then "raise the bar" again and again.

We believe that everything can be done better, faster, and more effectively in a learning environment.

■ *Individual Respect and Responsibility:* We will respect others and act responsibly, so that we can work together to meet our common goals.

■ *Innovation:* We will challenge conventional thinking, explore new technology, and implement new ideas, regardless of their source, faster than our competition.

■ *Integrity:* We will stand for honesty and trust in everything we do. We will say what we believe and do what we say.

■ *Teamwork:* We will win by thinking and acting together as one General Motors team, focused on global leadership. Our strengths are our highly skilled people and our diversity.[4]

Good Judgment and Common Sense

Joan Magretta in her previously mentioned book, *What Management Is: How It Works and Why It's Everyone's Business*, offers another illustration of the power of commitment to organizational values:

> At Southwest [Airlines], values are more important than rules ... [Southwest] created this plain-English statement of policy: "No employee will ever be punished for using good judgment and good old common sense when trying to accommodate a customer—no matter what our other rules are."[5]

Values are expressed through individual performance, as in respecting the rules, like Lehman and Mallon did; turning in a trophy you didn't really win; taking the proper actions when you are in the wrong place at the right time; putting family first like Phil, Johnny, and Ford; walking-the-talk; and establishing and living organization values like GE's, GM's, and Southwest's. In your job or career changes, have organization values played a role in your decisions? Will they if you change in the future?

The Sense of Integrity

The professional golfer's sense of integrity is enforced during tournament play because everyone is watching. Most weekend golfers are not held to the same standard. We often end up off the fairway where no one is watching. How many opportunities do we have to kick the ball out of the rough and improve our lie? Are we tempted to not count a whiff or topped shot that moves only a few feet? Our golf game often tests our personal honor. A little fudging is not a big deal. No one is hurt, right? Have you ever played with a "sandbagger" (cheater)? You see them adjusting their lie. You know they are not recording all their shots on the scorecard. What do you think of that person? Would you, or do you, trust them off the course?

The game of leadership is no different. Leaders often find themselves in the rough with no one watching. It's tempting to adjust the figures in a report to improve your lie. It won't hurt to take credit for work that isn't yours. We have seen the actions of leaders who lack the integrity to do the right thing in these and similar situations. How effective are they? How many actually get away with it? How do you feel about working with them, or working for them?

In golf, do you look for golfing partners with whom you have shared values? Are you most comfortable working with organizational colleagues who think as you do? Did you choose your organization because its culture, people, and policies are consistent with your values? Does your choice of values lead to satisfaction, enjoyment, and success in the games of golf and leadership?

Do your values also lead to a balanced perspective between work and play? You need to enjoy the game along the way—you know, catch the fragrance of the "greens."

Center Cut

Values define the fairways (boundaries of your actions), and create a comfortable environment of camaraderie, excitement, trust, and support for the achievement of success. The term "center cut" in golf identifies the position of a tee shot as being right in the middle of the fairway. It is never a bad place to be. Center-cut values can make you the kind of leader others want to follow and be like.

Solid values are the foundation for playing any game with integrity. They will be emphasized throughout our play on the Global Leadership Course. The role of the leader is to ensure that individual and organizational values are respected, prized, appreciated, and honored. Values-based leadership is virtuous leadership, a quality to strive for, an attribute as precious as diamonds. It is truly something to value.

The organizational policies and practices you establish or implement flow from underlying organizational and personal leadership values. So do the "rules of golf," which flow from the values inherent in the age-old game of golf, a topic we address on the next hole.

Character is what you do when no one else is looking.

Author Unknown

Quick Tips for Improving Your Leadership Game

Real leaders typically understand and model the following in their day-to-day actions:

- Serve your family.
  Serve your customers.
  Serve others.
  You'll do well in life.
- Take care of your people and they will take care of you. Not just those who follow you, but those who lead with you.
- Never say anything about a person who is not present that you would not say in that person's presence.
- Maintain the highest of ethical standards, that is, integrity, fairness, honesty, and a determination to do what's right.

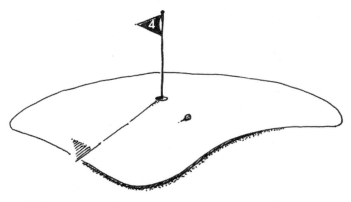

Play by the Rules

When the leader is morally weak and his discipline not strict, when his instructions and guidance are not enlightened, when there are no consistent rules, neighboring rulers will take advantage of this.

Sun Tzu, ancient Chinese philosopher

Malcolm Campbell, in his book *Ultimate Golf Techniques*, writes:

> To be a golfer rather than just a hitter of golf balls is to understand and respect the values that set the game of golf apart from all others. To play golf is to honor traditions and conventions echoed over five centuries, and to guard the spirit of fair, consistent and honest competition. . . . No other sport demands so much of its participants in terms of integrity.[1]

In a troubled world, the Rules of Golf remain perhaps the only code for which there is universal and voluntary acceptance.

A Golfer's Rules Wish List

The following seven rules appeared under the heading "The Rules of Golf" on a local computer bulletin board in Elkton, Maryland. An author was not credited, though we know of any number of golfers who could have written it.

■ *Rule 1.* "A ball sliced or hooked into the rough shall be lifted and placed in the fairway at a point equal to the distance it carried or rolled in the rough. Such veering right or left frequently results from friction between the face of the club and the cover of the ball, and the player should not be penalized for erratic behavior of the ball resulting from such uncontrollable mechanical phenomena."

■ *Rule 2.* "A ball hitting a tree shall be deemed not to have hit the tree. Hitting a tree is simply bad luck and has no place in the scientific game. The player should estimate the distance the ball would have traveled if it had not hit the tree and play the ball from there, preferably from a nice tuft of grass."

■ *Rule 3.* "There shall be no such thing as a lost ball. The missing ball is on or near the course somewhere and eventually will be found and pocketed by someone else. It thus becomes a stolen ball, and the player should not compound the felony by charging himself with a penalty stroke."

■ *Rule 4.* "If a putt passes over the hole without dropping, it is deemed to have dropped. The law of gravity holds that any object attempting to maintain a position in the atmosphere without something to support it must drop. The law of gravity supersedes the law of golf."

■ *Rule 5.* "Same thing for a ball that stops on the brink of the hole and hangs there defying gravity. You cannot defy the law."

■ *Rule 6.* "Same thing goes for a ball that rims the cup. A ball should not go sideways. This violates the laws of physics."

■ *Rule 7.* "A putt that stops close enough to inspire such comments as 'You could blow it in' may be blown in. This rule does not apply if the ball is more than three inches from the hole, because no one wants to make a travesty of the game."

The "Tuesday Group"

For many years on Tuesday mornings, when our Midwest weather permits, I have met with Bob Lauer (Mr. Navy), Ralph Rogers (Speedy), Vince Richard (One-Putt), Dick Rice (Smoothie), Stan Moyer (Laugh-A-Minute), and Dick Heckman (Lefty) for an early morning round of golf at historic Ottawa Park. Laid out in 1899, Ottawa Park is the oldest 18-hole public golf course west of New York. This narrow, rolling, tree-lined layout tests a golfer's accuracy. It is one of Toledo's most popular courses. We like it because it has a lot of character, and quite frankly is not as long as some other courses we might play.

The "Tuesday Group" does not follow the "rules" listed above. In deference to our senior amateur status, we make a few allowances. At each golfer's discretion, the option of one mulligan for front- and back-nine tee shots is granted. We also tend to be generous in the event of the nasty "unplayable lie," if relief is requested. We know the rules of golf. We also know we are playing the game for enjoyment and not to qualify for the Champions Tour. So, we have a few "gentlemen's agreements," which for our circumstance no less a golf traditionalist than Ben Crenshaw says are okay. But when we apply "our special rules" we also readily admit we are not playing to the "real rules of golf."

"Real golfers" play by the rules, albeit some with acceptable "gentlemen's agreements." Those who do not play by the rules—that is, those who cheat—are viewed with disdain. Those who attempt to make their scores appear better than they actually are rarely go undetected. Similarly, the leader who does not play by the rules is not exercising "real leadership" and is perceived a failed leader by his or her followers. Golf is an individual game, as is leadership. "I" is at the center of the word ethical, there is no they. Don't just talk a good game, play a good game.

Golf's Code of Rules

The Golfer's Home Companion[2] traces the rules of golf "back to 1744, when the Honourable Company of Edinburgh Golfers (the first known golf club, which is now located at Muirfield Golf Club, to the east of the Scottish capital) persuaded the city fathers to put up a trophy that members could compete for annually. To the Honourable Company, the 'Silver Club' meant formal recognition. But in order to stage the tournament equitably, the club had to draw up a code of conduct.

The first "Code of Rules" amounted to thirteen articles, and remarkably many of the original rules remain virtually unchanged today. However, more rules have been added over the years. *The Official Rules of Golf*, as approved and published by The United States Golf Association (USGA) and the Royal and Ancient Golf Club of St. Andrew, Scotland, now cover etiquette; definitions; the rules of play; teeing ground; playing the ball; the putting green; ball moved, deflected, or stopped; relief situations and procedure; other forms of play; administration; local rules; conditions of the competition; design of clubs; the ball; miscellaneous; and rules of amateur status.[3] The rules apply to all golfers, and are strictly adhered to by professionals and competitive amateurs. Golfers police the rules themselves. Only if there is a question of rule interpretation is a PGA official consulted.

As this is written, the PGA Tour is announcing a club-testing process to ensure the legality of the golf clubs being used in tour events. The spring-like effect of the new class of "hot" drivers has allowed many golfers to significantly improve their driving distance off the tee. Consequently, some people are questioning whether or not the USGA's club spring limitations are being met. All golf clubs and balls are required to meet established specifications, although golfers generally rely on their manufacturers to meet these requirements.

The PGA tour will begin using the new test in January of 2004. The test machine will be on-site at all PGA sponsored events. Interestingly, in keeping with the game's tradition of integrity, the test will not be mandatory. As always, the players are expected to be honest and to monitor themselves. Will there be a need for a whistle-blower? I don't think so.

Play by Your Own Rules?

Vince Flynn, in his national bestseller *Term Limits*, illustrates a different and all-too-often-held view of how to exercise the power placed in the hands of a leader:

Garret's plan was simple. All he had to do was continue to portray the president as a victim and hope those idiots over at the FBI could catch these people. He smiled at how easy it was to play the power game against principled men like Roach. While they took the time to decide if a course of action was right or wrong, Garret worried only about being caught. He had no time for petty little laws and technicalities, and he definitely had no time for someone else's morals. He was there to get things done, and to play by his own rules.[4]

People playing by their own rules can disrupt a game of golf. Leaders who play by their own rules, and not by those governing the rest of the organization, provide poor examples. Their actions can lead to less than optimum organizational performance.

When a new president was named to head a huge, world-wide merchandising organization, he told his new subordinates that it was now "his turn" to get the top executive perks. Just weeks after instituting a severe cost-cutting program across the organization, the president attended a large industry convention in San Francisco. He booked the finest suite in an expensive hotel. For his own purposes, he ordered underlings to install a large refrigerator in his suite.

When the refrigerator was delivered, it was too large to fit through the hotel room doorway. In order to comply with the president's demand, the staff arranged for a window in the 26th-floor suite to be removed and for the refrigerator to be lifted in through the window frame by a huge crane. At the end of the convention, the president simply left the unit in the hotel and went home.

Everyone in the company who knew about the refrigerator incident found little motivation to further cut any of their expenses. And you tell me, who in the company didn't hear the "refrigerator story?" Just as the rules of golf apply to all who play, there should not be a set of rules for the boss and a different set for other members of the organization. If there are, everybody loses.

It takes great courage to report misconduct on the golf course, and even more to do so within one's own organization. Whistle-blowers are given a very difficult time. In most cases, it is a David and Goliath scenario. Yet Cynthia Cooper of WorldCom, Coleen Rowley of the FBI, and Sherron Watkins of Enron—*Time* magazine's "2002 Persons of the Year"—took huge personal and professional risks to report what was wrong within their respective organizations. "In so doing," as reported in *Time*'s December 30, 2002 issue, "they helped remind us what American courage and American values are all about." They reminded all of us that it is the leaders' obligation, at all levels, to play by the rules and to exemplify the highest code of conduct.

It is unfortunate that we have seen, see, and will continue to see, people who play the leadership game by their own rules. Some even appear to get away with it. They adhere to the politics of personal power and not to the politics of the greater good. They are not real leaders but simply power brokers who by circumstance are able to wreak havoc on people and organizations until they are forced from their positions of power. Many of us at one time or another have been victims of this kind of person. Two questions:

1. Are you one of them?
2. Are you playing and/or tending to play the politics of personal power or the politics of the greater good?

And add a third question:

3. Do you sleep well at night?

The Rules Are for Everyone

Contrast the "refrigerator story" with the example of the outdoor furniture and accessories outlet owner who returned from lunch one day with his general manager. They noticed that the display lot was littered with paper and trash. This was despite the owner's insistence on clean, attractive premises. The general manager said she would immediately get the lot porter to clean up the debris.

The owner said no, and that he and the general manager would clean it up. He was fully aware that what they were doing would be reported within the ranks. Within minutes, the word spread through the grapevine to all 100 employees of the outlet that the "old man" really meant what he said about good housekeeping. It was everyone's job, even the owner's, not just that of the lowest paid person on the staff. Good example travels fast.

A Short Self-Assessment

In our leadership development and consulting work, we use the Adaptive Leader Skills Assessment (ALSA) to measure perceptions of a leader's effectiveness. The ALSA uses a forced distribution requirement to aid in the identification of a leader's more effective and less effective skills. The ALSA "ethics cluster" includes, among others, the five skills shown in Figure 4-1.

Scorecards are integral to the game of golf. They measure the golfer's performance level. I suggest you score yourself on your leadership ethics skills, using the scale shown in Figure 4-1. Using a forced distribution, rank order the skills from 5 (most effective) to 1 (least effective). Your scoring will provide a measurement of relative effectiveness on these skills.

These may be simple instructions, but if you scored yourself I suspect that it was somewhat difficult to work out the forced distribution. Hopefully, the process generated some thoughtful insights into your quest to be an even more ethical leader.

Now, if you are interested and brave enough, ask some of your colleagues or direct reports to rate you using the same forced distribution. Any difference between their perception of your ethical behavior and your own evaluation is important for you to know and analyze.

Why Be Ethical?

Why be ethical? Mark Roe and Jesper Parnevik were disqualified following the third round of the 2003 British Open, which was played in Sandwich, England on the Royal St. George's course.

FIGURE 4-1.
Sample leadership ethics assessment.

As a leader, I:

_____ Demonstrate trustworthiness.

_____ Give credit where credit is due.

_____ Promote what is right, not what is safe and easy.

_____ Model honesty.

_____ Demonstrate people matter to me.

Using a forced distribution, rank order the skills from 1 (least effective) to 5 (most effective), according to the following leadership effectiveness scale:

1—Least effective

2—Less effective

3—Acceptable

4—More effective

5—Most effective

SOURCE: Adaptive Leader Consulting Associates, Ltd., *Adaptive Leader Skills Assessment.* Copyright 1994.

The reason for the disqualification was that they failed to exchange scorecards at the first hole of play, as is the correct procedure. This meant that when they signed their cards at the end of the round they had signed for what were in effect their playing partner's scores, not their own. When they turned the cards in to the Royal and Ancient official scorers at the end of the round, the cards were checked and accepted as okay. However, after the golfers left the scorer's tent the error was discovered. The rule-making Royal and Ancient Club later accepted some blame for the official scorers not having detected the error when they reviewed the scorecards with the players. A special committee considered the possibility of waiving the rule and allowing Roe and Parnevik to play the fourth round, but decided against it. The responsibility for correct scoring was the golfers'. Roe had finished the round just three shots from the lead, and had a clear possibility of winning the Open, while Parnevik was 15 shots behind the leader. Later, an obviously disappointed but noncomplaining Roe told a news conference, "Rules are there to protect the game."

Ethical behavior protects the players in the leadership game, both leaders and followers. Ethics refers to the rules and guidelines of conduct by which we try to live. These underpin the relationships between people and their organizations. Leaders have the responsibility for upholding and fairly administering organizational rules, policies, and standards. Often these are not as simple and straightforward as the rules and courtesies of play associated with the game of golf. Rather, they are often complex in their application because we are required as leaders to make decisions that require balancing company needs with employee needs, budget goals, or business objectives while maintaining human goals, doing what's right for the greater good, and being tough yet fair and compassionate.

Survive the Cut

Leadership decisions can be difficult, even anguishing, at any level of the organization. A good ethical compass, a code of conduct, sound values and policies are all needed to guide the leader. Decisions made in difficult circumstance, if thoughtful and well intentioned, will generally come out just fine. Act with integrity, a sense of fairness, and a focus on doing what is right and you will sleep well at night.

The first objective of the professional or amateur golfer playing in a tournament is to "survive the cut." Thursday and Friday play determines who will play on the weekend. Approximately half of the starting field survives. The rest go home. The weekend players earn money whether they finish first or last. Those who don't qualify for Saturday and Sunday are shut out.

Organizations also need to play well against the competition, make the cut to survive, and strive to be at least among the best at the end of Sunday's play. Competition for survival and success is intense. New products and technologies come on the business scene just as increasing numbers of talented young players join the PGA Tour. Leaders must deal with new challenges to their organizations and with the impact they have on their followers.

Win or Lose, Respect the Game

I was part of such a "new" challenge at Owens-Illinois Incorporated (O-I) from 1986 to 1987. O-I was a successful company dating back to the 1920s. Its principal business historically was, and still is, glass container packaging. O-I was an original member of the Dow 30. A paternalistic company from the start, O-I was a highly ethical company that placed high value on its employees and their welfare. O-I was in the top 80 of the Fortune 100 in sales, and in the top 40 in number of employees.

In 1986, senior O-I executives entered discussions about "taking O-I private" with Kohlberg, Kravis, and Roberts (KKR), a New York investment banking firm. Following a back-and-forth of alternative strategies, a KKR offer was judged to be the best shareholder value, and O-I went private in 1987.

In 1988, O-I was a leaner, more efficient organization. It had reduced layers of management, gotten out of poor-return-on-investment holdings, and was focused on its core business. The leaders of O-I, up and down the line, were dramatically impacted by the changes in the company. As the efforts to make and keep O-I competitive moved forward, many employees of all ages were devastated as they lost their jobs and their dream of long-term job security. It was a very difficult, emotion-filled time for those staying as well as those leaving.

I was proud of the way the organization offered help to people and of the actions of front-line leaders, who fairly and thoughtfully dealt with the individual trauma of severe workforce reduction. Efforts included offering early retirement programs, special payment opportunities for those not eligible for retirement, employee counseling, resume and job placement services, and health benefit continuation. Every effort was made to help people work through individual hardships. Front-line leadership handled difficult, even agonizing situations and did so professionally. They demonstrated the ability to balance the needs of the business with the individual needs of their employees. They showed that they were "real leaders."

A senior O-I executive summed up the O-I struggle with change with this personal perspective. "When I left O-I in 1988, I liked the company less than I had in 1962 when I joined it, but I respected it more. The international economy and rapidly changing technology had forced change. A series of capable CEOs and COOs had directed the change and done it well. Personally, I had made a good living, had enjoyed my work for the most part, felt I had contributed significantly to the progress of O-I, and got to know some of the finest people in the world."

Win or lose, you should respect the game. Be proud of how well you play and what you achieve. And respect and enjoy your playing partners in the leadership game.

It is critical for you, for all leaders, to have a personal code of conduct and to perform to a high ethical standard. Your followers expect and deserve no less from you than integrity, fairness, honesty, trust, and the determination to do what's right. Such behavior is a requirement of leadership excellence on a personal level. Remember you are always under the microscope of your observant colleagues at all levels. As an automotive parts plant manager liked to remind his people, "You are about to take an action you are not convinced is the right thing to do. Stop, and ask yourself, if I do this will I mind if it is reported as a front page headline in tomorrow morning's newspaper?"

Rules and codes of conduct can be viewed as limiting, and they certainly are. They can also be viewed as defining the game, making it unique from other activities. This is true both of the game of golf and of the game of leadership, though the rules of the latter are not so clearly defined as they are in golf.

Learn What Not to Do

One of the realities of leadership is that some of the most powerful lessons learned are "what not to do" rather than "what to do."

After all, if you at least know what not to do you shouldn't be making that mistake. Leaders have provided case studies of what not to do for centuries. Consider what Cicero wrote 2000 years ago:

The Six Mistakes of Man

1. The delusion that personal gain is made by crushing others.
2. The tendency to worry about things that cannot be changed or corrected.
3. Insisting that a thing is impossible because we cannot accomplish it.
4. Refusing to set aside trivial preferences.
5. Neglecting development and refinement of the mind, and not acquiring the habit of reading and studying.
6. Attempting to compel others to believe and live as we do.

Sound familiar? Ever make any of these mistakes? Are you making any of them now?

Learn What to Do

Here's another list of actions. I've developed this list based on my experiences and my observations of "real leaders," intent on effectively and ethically playing the leadership game.

Real Leaders

1. Envision and pursue the greater good.
2. Ethically and enthusiastically excite, educate, empower, enable, and expect.
3. Realistically control and/or influence.
4. Pursue the six C's: caring, credible, committed, consistent, confident, and courageous.

5. Treat people as adults.

6. Trust first and be trustworthy.

7. Read to lead and walk-the-talk.

8. Listen, listen, listen and then ask one more question.

9. Intuitively generate adaptive change.

10. Go to their kid's ball games!

How does this list compare to your rules for the game of leadership? What is your code of conduct? What guides your leadership actions? Are you approaching the game of leadership with the same integrity as you approach the game of golf? Just as in the game of golf, only *you* know your real score!

The Guy in the Glass

Peter "Dale" Wimbrow, Sr. wrote the poem *The Guy in the Glass* in 1934. It was published in the *American Magazine* at that time. Over the years the poem has appeared under incorrect titles, such as "The Man in the Glass," or "The Face in the Glass." Since it was written, the poem has taken on a life of its own and is often followed by the notation, "author unknown." Some people have even assigned their name to the poem and misquoted the original.

Sallydale Wimbrow and Peter Dale Wimbrow, Jr. established a computer Web site in 1997, "The Official Guy in the Glass Web Page." They did so because they are immensely proud of their father's work and wanted to, in their words, "set the record straight and to provide the poem as it was actually written for any and all to use as our father's gift to the world. . . . He would have wanted his work to be a gift and so do we. All we ask is that you properly credit him somewhere in your publication as the author."

Here is the original poem and its clear message. Incidentally, a word in the poem most often changed is "pelf," which appears in the first line. "Self" is substituted. But for those of us who pursue careers in business, pelf is a most appropriate word. You probably don't need to look it up, but if you are stumped, as I was, "pelf" means "money or wealth."

> ### The Guy in the Glass
> *When you get what you want in your struggle for pelf,*
> *And the world makes you "King for a Day,"*
> *Then go to the mirror and look at yourself,*
> *And see what that guy has to say.*
>
> *For it isn't your Father or Mother or Wife*
> *Who judgment upon you must pass,*
> *The feller whose verdict counts most in your life*
> *Is the guy staring back from the glass.*
>
> *He's the feller to please, never mind the rest,*
> *For he's with you clear up to the end;*
> *And you've passed your most dangerous, difficult test*
> *If the guy in the glass is your friend.*
>
> *You may be like Jack Horner and "chisel" a plum,*
> *And think you're a wonderful guy,*
> *But the man in the glass says you're only a bum*
> *If you can't look him straight in the eye.*
>
> *You can fool the whole world down the pathway of years,*
> *And get pats on the back as you pass,*
> *But your final reward will be heartache and tears,*
> *If you've cheated the guy in the glass.*[5]

Quick Tips for Improving Your Leadership Game

Real leaders typically understand and model the following in their day-to-day actions:

- Nice gals and guys do not finish last!
- Tell the truth, then you don't have to remember anything.
- Always do what you say you are going to do and you will be respected.

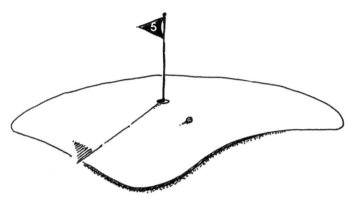

Tee It Up with Vision

Vision without action is merely a dream. Action without vision just passes the time. Vision with action can change the world.[1]

Joel Barker, *The Power of Vision* (video)

Bob Frosch came to General Motors from NASA in the late 1980s to become the first technical head in its history to be hired from outside the corporation. His title was vice president, GM Research Laboratories. Bob enjoyed telling the following story:

One evening in the late 1960s, as Frosch was walking through one of NASA's buildings on his way to the parking lot, he came upon a janitor sweeping in the aisles. The janitor was whistling a happy tune as he pushed his broom. Bob greeted him:

"Hi, how're you doing?"

"Doing great. And you, sir?"

``Just fine. You seem to be enjoying your work.''

``Oh, you bet'' replied the janitor, ``I love my job.''

``Well, that's terrific,'' said Bob, ``what are you going to be doing tonight?''

``Helping put a man on the moon, sir, helping put a man on the moon.''

The janitor knew specifically what NASA's vision was at the time and clearly it was inspiring to him. Visions are supposed to provide direction and inspiration.

A Brief Exercise

It is obvious that I cannot see you. Nonetheless, I have a request that shows my trust in you. I think you will find the following brief exercise interesting and beneficial.

Please do this exercise before reading the paragraphs following this one. I'm going to ask you to close your eyes for about sixty seconds while visualizing your favorite vacation spot. Go there in your mind's-eye. See yourself doing the things you enjoy doing with the people you know and love. Easy enough? Okay, close your eyes for about sixty seconds and visit your favorite vacation place!

Ah, you're back, safe and sound. If you fell asleep, now that you are rested, go back to the previous paragraph and try again! If you succeeded with your visualization, I am certain you enjoyed it. Here are a couple of questions for you:

1. Did you have any trouble visualizing your favorite vacation spot?

2. Could you see yourself there, doing the things you like to do, with the people you enjoy most?

3. Did you have a clear black-and-white picture?

People invariably say no to number 1, yes to number 2, and for number 3 they adamantly declare NO, it was in Technicolor! How about you?

The foregoing simple visualization exercise illustrates the clarity and power of positive mental images.

Focusing back on your leadership role, here are a few more questions for you:

1. Is your organization's vision clear to you? Is it in black-and white or Technicolor?

2. Is your vision of your leadership role in support of the organization's vision clear to you? Black-and-white or Technicolor?

3. Have you delivered your and the organization's vision to those for whom you are responsible as a leader? Yes or no? If yes, do they see it in black-and-white or Technicolor?

4. Finally, do you have a vision for yourself and your future in the game of leadership, much as Woods, Sorenstam, and the other stars of the sport have for their future in the game of golf?

Leadership Is Poetry

Leadership is more than technique, though techniques are necessary. In a sense, management is prose; leadership is poetry. The leader necessarily deals to a large extent in symbols, in images, and in the sort of galvanizing idea that becomes a force of history. People are persuaded by reason, but moved by emotion; the leader must both persuade them and move them. The administrator thinks of yesterday and today. The manager thinks of yesterday, today, and tomorrow. The leader thinks of yesterday, today, and tomorrow but focuses on the day after tomorrow.

It is not enough for the leader to know the right thing. The leader must also be able to do the right thing. The would-be leader without the judgment or perception to make the right decisions fails for lack of vision. The one who knows the right thing but cannot achieve it is ineffectual and fails. Vision is not restricted to the leaders at the top of the organization. It's a requirement for success at every level, not only in your vocational life, but in your private life as well. The old cliché is so true, "If you don't know where you are going, any road will get you there."

Vision or Mission

Vision statements are sometimes confused with mission statements. Let me end the confusion for you. A "vision statement" is what causes you to go to sleep at night with a smile on your face. A "mission statement" causes you to get up in the morning and work at attaining the vision.

We talked about values at hole #2. Vision statements are value statements, and together with mission statements they can provide clear over-arching direction to your activities as a leader. The mission statements can help you and your people to focus on the part of the vision that you can impact. My favorite mission statement is one used by a Canadian marketing organization, "Easy to buy, a pleasure to own." I don't see where there would be too many questions regarding what is meant by that? And, more importantly, it clearly and concisely tells the members of the marketing staff what their responsibility is to the customer.

Connecting Vision and Values to the Bottom Line

Senior leaders have a broad view of the organization's strategy. The front-line workers know a lot of detail about their specific assignments and are at the pay point of the organization's activities. It is the job of the "leaders in the middle" to knit these two elements together.

Organizational vision and values are established by the top of the organization. They are translated into systems and structures that are intended to guide the organization's efforts in the direction of the vision and in a manner compatible with the values. These systems and structures can be well articulated and clearly understood, and are expected to be practiced and followed by everyone. Or, they can get distorted and take the organization off track.

The behaviors thus inspired dictate the daily decisions made and the consequent success or failure in achieving the vision. Figure 5-1 illustrates the connection of vision and values to the bottom line.

President John F. Kennedy expressed the vision of putting a man on the moon. One of his reasons was to reinvigorate the value of being an American. The systems and structure of NASA together with the daily decisions of all the people involved in the vision brought success. Most Americans alive at the time heard Neil Armstrong's historic communication from the moon to mission control Houston as the vision was achieved. That adventure perfectly illustrates the power of a vision to inspire people to do the seemingly impossible.

The Visualization Process

Visualization with action can lead to achievement in space, on the golf course, and in the game of leadership. There are at least four

FIGURE 5-1.
Vision links top-line values to the bottom line.

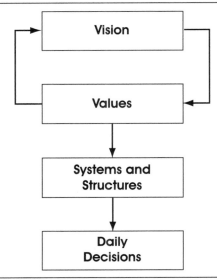

points to keep in mind with regard to your process of visualization:

1. First, visualize yourself succeeding and what success will look like for you. For example, do you see yourself as a concert pianist, a skilled cabinet maker, a licensed physical therapist, a professional golfer, or a respected leader?

2. Next, visualize the benefits that will flow from being successful in achieving your vision. What benefits are important to you? Are they professional recognition, helping others succeed, money, status, security for yourself and your family, etc.?

3. Your visualization will need to be sustained over time. Its sustaining power can come from continuing affirmations. You will need to "talk to yourself" and talk in the present tense, as in "I practice everyday" instead of "I will practice everyday." For example, I became interested in running for exercise long before it became a fitness rage. My colleagues were not into exercise. They were constantly asking whether I was still doing that running thing. I made it a point, for my affirmation and motivation, to respond in the following fashion. "I ran three miles this morning. It was great and I'll be running again tomorrow morning. I'll take the weekend off and be back at it again on Monday morning. You should try it." I ran for years until my knees said, "no more." I still miss it, but now I walk the dog.

4. Visions are rarely fulfilled in one dramatic moment but rather only after reaching a series of attainable goals. Neil Armstrong did not reach the moon in a single launch. Rather a whole series of space experiments provided the knowledge, experience, and equipment necessary for the moon landing. Similarly, Tiger Woods did not win the four major professional championships— the Masters, U.S. Open, British Open, and PGA Championship— all at once. He had to visualize winning each in its own time. In the process, he did what no other golfer has been able to do, which is to hold all four major titles at the same time. I don't know whether Tiger envisioned the "Tiger Slam," but I imagine he did. I do know he won them one at a time. And I believe that he has both a visualization to be the greatest golfer ever to play the game and a series of goals he sees as necessary affirmations along the way.

If you have committed to being a leader, a real leader, you first need to visualize what kind of leader you want to be. Only then can you begin thinking about what you need and want to do to reach your goal.

Joel Barker, in his excellent video, *The Power of Vision*, presents research that young people of lesser intelligence who have a vision of what it is they want to accomplish tend to outperform those who have greater intelligence but no clear direction. A clear vision of a goal sets a positive and comfortable stage for our actions regardless of our age. As Aristotle said, "The soul never thinks without a picture."

According to Dr. Deborah Graham, who works with over 200 PGA, LPGA, Champions, and Buy.com Tour players on the mental approach to the game:

> In golf, your objective on the first tee, as with all other shots, should be to keep your body relaxed, your mind quiet, and your focus narrow so that you will have the best chance to use your skills. The quality of your mental routine (your commitment to your shot, your image of what you want the ball to do and your feel for the tempo you want) will strongly influence the quality of your shot.[2]

And so it is with leadership and your actions as leader.

Organization Vision: Clear to Everyone?

Leaders too often fail to make the organization vision clear to everyone and, worse, send very clear messages that establish a wrong direction for individual action.

In one U.S. Army unit stationed in Germany, little effort was given to identifying the unit's mission and how it fit into the Army's overall vision and values. Few seemed to know exactly why they were assigned in Germany or what it was they needed to accomplish. The rank-and-file troops were not aware of how their individual performance affected unit performance. They simply responded to the pressures of the last order received.

A tank driver in that unit was experiencing bad radio communications. The reason for the difficulty was that his tank radio antenna was corroded and bent. He had a good antenna stored away in his tank but he was saving it! He was saving it for the next company commander inspection, because he had once been chewed out at inspection for having a corroded antenna. He had "learned" that clean equipment for inspections was more important than good communications on the battlefield.

Another example involves a railroad switching yard. Switching yards are busy places and can be dangerous. At that time, the switching yard controls were located in a glassed-in booth overlooking the yard. The operator was a long-service employee. His job was critical in maintaining safe conditions in the yard. Safety is the number one concern in any workplace, and it was certainly part of the vision management held for operation of the switching yard.

One warm, sunny day, a consultant, hired by management to review the railroad's operations, climbed to the top of the switching yard tower to talk with the tower operator. As he entered the operator's booth, he observed the operator straining on one of the brakes used to control switching operations. The brake shuddered, seemed to slip, then grabbed, after which the operator released his grip on it. Perspiration dripped from the operator's face. The consultant said:

> "Wow, that looked tough. Is that brake supposed to work like that?"
>
> "Of course not. The pads are worn and one of these days it's going to fail and we'll have a big mess in the yard."
>
> "Have you reported this to management?"
>
> "No, and I don't plan to either."
>
> Not believing what he had just heard, the consultant asked, "Why not?"

``Well, you see the glass windows all around this booth? The sun comes in and heats this place like an oven.'' (As he spoke, the operator took a handkerchief out of his pocket and wiped the perspiration from his face.) ``Now, I've told my boss and sent four memos to management asking for some blinds for these windows, and maybe a fan, and haven't gotten the first response. The way I figure it, when someone talks to me about the blinds and the fan, I'll tell them about the brakes!''

The tank commander and the switching-yard operator had gotten the wrong message about vision and value, courtesy of management. Leaders must align with stated visions and values and reinforce them with their daily decisions. That's the bottom line.

Something Significant Yet to Do

Viktor Frankl, in his classic work about survival in the World War II Nazi concentration camps, *Man's Search for Meaning*, writes that those who survived shared one common focus, each had "something significant yet to do in the future."[3] They had a vision. The leader needs that kind of direction and so do his or her followers. Frankl not only survived Auschwitz, he became, along with Freud and Adler, the most famous of the Viennese psychotherapists. *Man's Search for Meaning* sold more than 2 million copies, is in its seventy-third edition, and has been translated into twenty-six languages. Victor Frankl is not likely to be soon forgotten.

According to Frankl, mental health is about looking forward, not backward, and about finding purpose in life. It is about having a positive vision of the future. Frankl lived on his visions long after relying on them to give him the mental strength to survive Auschwitz. He died a few years ago at age 92.

There are many stories of people surviving the most difficult of circumstances by visualizing those things having significant meaning to them. One such story involved an American prisoner of war during the Korean War, who was imprisoned for more than five years. One of his avocations before his capture was the game of golf. In fact, he was a very good player, a scratch golfer. Finally, he was released from captivity and, as you would expect, he spent several months going through a rehabilitation process to regain his health and strength. At the very first opportunity, he played a round of golf. He shot 74. His partners were amazed and asked him how he had been able to do so well. And he told them, "It wasn't hard at all. I've been playing today's round every day for the past five years!"

A "visioning technique" that some people use is to write the speech they would like to hear at their retirement party, or perhaps to write their own obituary. The purpose is to capture the vision of future successes that the person will then strive to accomplish.

Finally, you need to ensure that your visualizations are realistic and doable. If they are not, change them to what is doable, with a stretch, and maintain a positive, optimistic view of the future.

Winston Churchill, one of my favorite historical leaders, was literally an "eternal optimist" who held positive visions of the future. He prescribed his own funeral arrangements, which were followed at his actual funeral service at London's St. Paul's Cathedral. There were two buglers, located at opposite ends of the church. At the close of the ceremony, the first bugler, at the front of the church, played "Taps." Just before he finished, and as Churchill's casket reached the doors of the church, the second bugler began to play "Reveille."

Why is it the ship beats the waves when the waves are so many and the ship is one? The reason is that the ship has a purpose.

Winston Churchill

Quick Tips for Improving Your Leadership Game

Real leaders typically understand and model the following in their day-to-day actions:

- Explain the organization's vision to your associates in your own words without reference to the vision document and translate it into day-to-day actions related to your leadership responsibilities.

- Use the components of the vision as key criteria in assessing alternatives, in making decisions, and in challenging actions, or lack of action, not consistent with the vision.

- A lesson from Noah's Ark: Build your future on high ground.

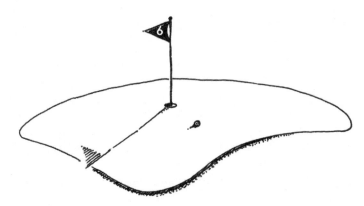

Posture, Grip, Alignment (PGA)

To get an elementary grasp of the game of golf, a human must learn, by endless practice, a continuous and subtle series of highly unnatural movements involving about sixty-four muscles, that result in a seemingly "natural swing," taking all of two seconds to begin and end.[1]

Alistair Cooke, British journalist

Effective leadership starts with a strong foundation. We've discussed three of the four corners essential to your leadership foundation. On hole #3, we talked about policies and practices that reflect the values of the organization and the importance of your personal values. As we teed up on the next hole, we stressed the need to play by the rules of ethics, honor, and organizational standards. And on the hole we just played, we discussed the necessity for you and your followers to be able to pursue a vision that provides a clear, over-arching direction to your leadership activity and their efforts.

Each of these requirements for play is found in both the game of golf and the game of leadership. Hopefully, as we have played these holes you've identified any deficiencies that you need to address. Even more hopefully, you feel good about where you stand on values, rules, and vision. I know you are itching to make improvements as we continue the round, but first we need to consider the fourth corner of our foundation.

The game of golf relies on the effective application of posture, grip, and alignment, which means properly setting up to effectively swing the club and play the game. A myriad of seemingly different applications of these elements can be observed as we watch golf on television or observe other players as we play our local courses. Some work well, others do not. And, it is easy to tell what works and what doesn't, because the results are clearly observable to all. Those results are traceable to whether or not there is appropriate application of the fundamentals of posture, grip, and alignment. I know you've observed the acronym, PGA.

Posture, grip, and alignment combine to provide the golfer with the proper setup for playing the game. On this hole let's examine how the golfer prepares to swing effectively and compare that to what you as a leader need to do in final preparation for swinging the leadership club. It is probably not necessary to get as basic as UCLA's basketball coaching great, John Wooden, who is reported to have taught his players how to play the game by first teaching them how to lace up and tie their shoes. But it is necessary for you to feel comfortable with your leadership footing.

Posture (A Realistic Stance)

The revered golfing figure, Bobby Jones, once commented, "The general criticisms which are to be made of the average player's posture at address are that his feet are too far apart, his body is bent too much, and his arms are extended too far."[2] Posture to the golfer means the proper positioning of the various body parts for comfort, leverage, and ease of swing. The golfer wants to be sure of a solid base to work from, and so positioning is very important. The fundamentals of correct golfing posture involve slightly bending the knees, a forward tilt at the hips, a straight back, and body weight evenly distributed between the toes and balls of the feet. The purpose is to establish a realistically sound athletic approach to the golf stance. Leaders need to develop a realistic stance regarding their leadership play on the Global Leadership Course.

A realistic stance for the leader must consider a variety of elements. How are you positioning yourself as a leader in the organization? What direction is the organization heading? What are the requirements for success in running your business today, tomorrow, and the day after tomorrow? What do you see as your role in helping to lead the organization? Is it the need to be a dynamic leader, a tough-minded boss, a developmental mentor and coach, a turn-around expert, a consensus builder, a micromanager, or a facilitator? Have you made the diagnosis and verified it so that your leadership posture fits the demands of the situation you have been assigned? Is your organization playing in the fairway, out of the rough, on the upslope of growth or the downslope of down-sizing? Wow! Yes, you have to do this analysis of your business and organization setting before expecting to play the leadership game effectively.

Success at golf, leadership, or any endeavor of substance requires that we understand and play within the realities of the environment. Golfers understand this, and the good ones pursue a well-thought-out course management strategy, which includes consideration of the layout of each hole on the golf course. Distance, slope, rough, width of fairways, location of water hazards and sand traps, and pin placements are all considered. Then adjustments are made to respond to the vagaries of the weather and the potential effect of wind, rain, early morning dew, afternoon drying-out, and so on. Course management is serious business to the wise golfer. It is part of posturing to play the golf course.

Similarly, understanding the leadership course environment

is serious business for the wise leader. The twenty-first century already is, and promises to continue to be, one of great complexity and challenge. You need a sound and realistic view of the overall situational environment to play the leadership game. The Global Leadership Course is one tough layout!

The Leadership Environment

At one of the previously mentioned "Leadership NOW" (L-NOW) sessions I conducted within General Motors, I had the pleasure of meeting and working with Bob Dorn, then chief engineer for GM's Cadillac Division. Bob was a highly respected engineer, a great person, and a real leader. I vividly remember his taking over an L-NOW session one afternoon. He politely asked the facilitators to hand over the chart pads and marking pens, and to find a comfortable seat. Bob then proceeded to present his fellow leaders, and yours truly, a fundamental lesson regarding the leadership environment for then and for the foreseeable future.

Bob was a student of military history. He began his conversation by drawing on a chart pad an organizational pyramid and the communication/information flow arrows for a hierarchical organization such as GM. As shown in Figure 6-1, the dominating big arrow moves from top to bottom, and a set of small arrows moves from the bottom to the top. GM was, and historically had been, a model for the top-down hierarchical organization. Top leaders provided vision, values, and strategies, and they were supported by middle management, first-line supervision, and hundreds of thousands of front-line workers.

On another chart pad, Bob then drew a pyramid similar to the one in Figure 6-1. He drew the same set of arrows on the second pyramid but labeled the organization as the U.S. Marine Corps. Bob pointed out that GM and the military were the classic models of hierarchical organization structure taught in colleges and universities. In Figure 6-2 we see the vision, values, and strategies of the generals and top brass, supported by officers, noncommissioned officers, and front-line marines.

But, Bob wasn't done. On a third chart pad, he drew yet an-

FIGURE 6-1.
Corporate communication flow: General Motors.

Vision/Values/Strategy

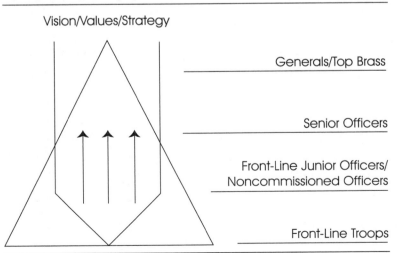

Chairman/CEO/Top Management

Middle Management

First-Line Supervision

Front-Line Workers

FIGURE 6-2.
Peacetime military communication flow: U.S. Marine Corps.

Vision/Values/Strategy

Generals/Top Brass

Senior Officers

Front-Line Junior Officers/
Noncommissioned Officers

Front-Line Troops

other illustration. This drawing, shown in Figure 6-3, is an inverted pyramid, with the Marine Corps hierarchy also inverted. But here the communication arrows point in the same direction as in Figures 6-1 and 6-2.

Bob then commented that the Marine Corps always responds to the environment. Figure 6-2, he explained, represents the Marine Corps functioning in an environment of peace—much the same as a GM or other business organization operates in a period of industry dominance. Figure 6-3 is the Marine Corps operating in a wartime environment.

In peacetime, the Marine Corps' generals and top leadership are able to dominate the communication flow and survive, much the same as a GM could when the competition was not strong and customers were satisfied. In wartime, the pyramid flips, and success in battle, meaning survival and victory, depends on the communication flow from platoon leaders and noncommissioned

FIGURE 6-3.
Wartime military communication flow: U.S. Marine Corps.

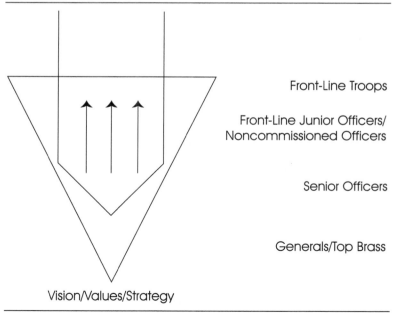

Front-Line Troops

Front-Line Junior Officers/
Noncommissioned Officers

Senior Officers

Generals/Top Brass

Vision/Values/Strategy

officers (NCOs) at the forward edge of the battle area (FEBA), and the responsive support of the leadership up the line. In short, survival and victory depend on the recognition that in war, leadership's role is to provide the support necessary for the front-line warriors to win the fire fights, the battles, and the war.

And then, Bob Dorn asked this question, "Is GM at war or at peace?"

It has been fifteen years since Bob Dorn delivered his lesson. I will leave it to you to judge the truth of his lesson today. For my part, the lesson is even more meaningful now. We need leaders who recognize that there is global competition in virtually every form of enterprise. That is the reality you face, today and in the future. Leaders need to view their role, not as one of power and authority, but as one of service and support. The main mission is to ensure that front-line workers receive the support necessary to succeed. As Winston Churchill said, "Support is the long green stem without which the bright flower of victory cannot bloom." And he added, "For without victory there is no survival."

Making the Cut

When leaders are asked the question, "What is the goal of a capitalist enterprise?" the answers are usually "to make money," "to reward the stockholders," or "to grow the business." Few, very few, respond as did John Smale, former CEO of Procter and Gamble and then chairman of GM's board, in a 1996 *Fortune* magazine article about the future of General Motors:

> A large capitalist enterprise must also be about higher goals than merely serving stockholders. A corporation is a human enterprise. It's not just a bunch of assets. The obligation of management is to perpetuate the corporation, which precedes their obligation to shareholders.[3]

Professional golf is also about survival. Only those "making the cut" get a pay day. The reality of organization life is that effective leadership is a must for "making the cut": achieving success and a long-term existence. This requires a solid grip on reality.

Get a Grip (Hands-On Principles)

Television analyst and Champions Tour player Gary McCord says, "You can fake anything, but a bad grip will follow you to the grave." Grip for the golfer is the proper placement of the hands on the golf club. The fundamental grip taught is an interlocking or overlapping of the hands in a relatively neutral position with the palm of the right hand (for right-handers) and the back of the left hand facing the target. One hand should not dominate the other. There are various grip applications, such as strong, weak, neutral, baseball, cross-handed, and motorcycle (the left hand and right hand are turned almost under the club, like twisting the throttle of a motorcycle).

Check Your Grip

You can't play good golf without a solid grip. You can't be a good leader without a solid grip on principles. You function as a leader on a basic set of principles. Even if you can't recite them for us, you have them. It is important for your success that they be good, solid principles. How about comparing your set of leadership operating principles to the following:

1. Always focus on the situation, issue, problem, decision, or behavior, and not on the person. (The golfer knows it is foolhardy to focus on anything other than the next shot.)

2. Maintain not only your own self-confidence but the self-confidence and self-esteem of others.

3. Maintain constructive relationships within your 360-degree sphere of influence.

4. Take the initiative to make things better. (Golfers constantly seek to improve.)

5. Always try doing the right thing as well as doing things right. (The golfer, with each shot, is faced with the decision of what is the right club and then must make the right swing to make the best shot.)

There is debate over whether or not leadership can be taught. Nonetheless, we know it can be learned. There are some fundamental leadership practices, just as there are in golf. Learn and practice these fundamentals. You must work at them. The tendency for many of us is to think that we are leadership "experts." Try to put this tendency aside and truly listen to those around you and continually question your leadership posture and grip for reinforcement and improvement.

B.C. Forbes' comments in the October 7, 1996 issue of *Forbes* make a powerful point for those who would lead in a global marketplace:

> We sometimes receive letters from businessmen who say they are "too busy to read." The man who is "too busy to read" is never likely to lead. The executive who aspires to success must keep himself well informed. His reading must not be confined to the reports of his own business laid on his desk, or to strictly trade journals, or to newspaper headlines. He must study what is going on throughout his own country and throughout the world. He must not remain blind to financial, industrial, economic trends, evolutions, revolutions.[4]

Alignment (Accuracy)

In *Ultimate Golf Techniques,* Malcolm Campbell comments on alignment: "If a gun is not aimed correctly, the bullet will not hit the target, and this principle applies just as much to the golf swing. The club face must be aimed at the target and the alignment of the body must match the angle of the club face—known as perfect parallel alignment."[5]

The recommended alignment resembles a railroad track. One track is the path from the ball on the tee and from the club face to the target. The other track is a parallel alignment of the shoulders, hips, and feet. There is a tendency to want to point the shoulders, hips, and feet at the target. It feels wrong not to do so, but as is true of pilots, you need to trust your instruments.

The leader needs to trust the instruments as well. You might refer to this as a bringing together of the elements of the game, whether golf or leadership, for a shot at the target. All the pieces—values, rules, vision, reality, and principles—are brought into alignment. The leader's task is to create this alignment. You can consider yourself the conductor of the orchestra, baton in hand, ready to play a leadership symphony.

Butch Harmon, David Leadbetter, and other skilled teachers are able to help professional golfers by identifying problems with their posture, grip, and alignment, and by suggesting corrections. The golfer must then translate these corrections into action. Who helps the leader in today's organizations identify his or her fundamental leadership problems? Sadly, there is not much help available beyond descriptions of leadership style and/or personality. What aspiring leaders need is "posture, grip, and alignment" assistance so they can determine how to improve their leadership effectiveness. They need the example and hands-on coaching of upper-level leaders, not the platitudes of surrogate facilitators and trainers inexperienced in leadership.

How Stupid Is This?

A union member, charged with coordination of an hourly-employee communication program sponsored by both union and management, made this observation: "Young people join the company. They've got good educations. They're assigned as first-line supervisors. There is no plan for these assignments. They go where the opening exists. It's luck of the draw whether or not they are assigned to a developmental manager who does things right. Now these young people take their lead from and try to emulate the behavior of their bosses. After all, they right away say to themselves, 'I want the bosses' job.' So, they become victims of the serendipity of the process, or lack of it. People on the line see this and say, 'how stupid is this!' "

Too often managers, and managements, express through their actions that leadership skills are innate, God-given, and don't have to be developed and directed. Others don't grasp the difference between power and authority. Some managers seem to believe their leadership skills are impeccable, or almost so. They could be improved somewhat but only if done so at little cost and minimal investment of time. Golfers are faced with similar assessments of their golfing skill. Of the two groups, only golfers seem willing to invest in improvement. Small wonder then that young people are not schooled in the fundamentals of leadership in their new organization environments but rather are handled as our coordinator of hourly employees observed.

Support for Alignment

GE's former chairman, Jack Welch, has expressed the view that the principal job of the leader is to develop other leaders. A vital part of the leader's role is to get a solid grip on the business, the organization's systems and structures, and the competition. Then he or she needs to align the organization's functions, systems, departments, and human resources so that they can be accurately driven, pitched, and putted at the assigned target. So, leaders need to be teachers. Teachers, to be successful, must spend time with their students and ensure they are taught the right things. And they need to start with a solid fundamental setup.

On occasion, I have facilitated a program titled "Fast Start," a product of Blessing/White, Inc. The idea of the program is to set up a fast-start discussion between a manager and a new supervisor/leader. Each of them is asked to independently assess the new leader's job priorities, group purpose(s), and required skills. This should take each of them approximately one hour. The new leaders then attend a one-half day workshop wherein they compare their job analysis with that of their manager's. This provides them an initial understanding of critical job skills, the manager's expectations, and how their strengths can contribute to the new assignment. A discussion plan is developed and meetings are scheduled with the new leader's manager to clarify any questions regarding job skills, expectations, use of strengths, etc.

Sound like a good idea? Meets the criteria of minimal time and cost! Well, in my experience, approximately one-third of managers, so-called leaders, do not complete and submit their pre-workshop material, another one-third provide incomplete responses, and only the remaining one-third take the process seriously. The potential leaders, with rare exception, come to the workshop prepared.

So, in two-thirds of the eighty to ninety cases I've observed, managers were unwilling, unable, uncaring, unbelieving, or just too lazy to prioritize the opportunity to support their new associates in a most fundamental way, getting off to a fast and good start. They are out of alignment. No facilitator can undo the message sent by these so-called leaders. Talk about a "values" message!

While he was CEO of General Electric, Jack Welch invested considerable time at GE's leadership development facility in Crotonville, New York. He fully understood, and exemplified, the importance of being a teacher and helping his organization's leaders to get their leadership posture and grip properly developed, and to get their leadership efforts correctly aligned with the corporate vision, values, strategies, and goals.

The Common Sense Club

Golf is a thinking person's game. You can do more to lower your score (handicap) by using your head than anything else. Before every shot, examine your options. What clubs could you use, what types of shots could you hit, what are the possible target areas. If your chances of a successful shot with one option are 3 in 10, and with another 8 in 10, then as a general rule you'd naturally go with the better percentage shot. In planning a shot, always try to set up the next shot, as in the game of pool. The "common sense" club—which is not the club of choice often enough for golfers or for leaders alike—needs to be played much more often. Just playing this club will decrease your golf score and increase your leadership effectiveness.

WHIFFs

Now that you have checked out your setup for playing the games of golf and leadership, a word of warning. The most unsuccessful golf swing is the WHIFF. Every golfer has experienced it. If you don't golf, a WHIFF is when you swing at the ball and completely miss it. Happens in baseball too. It results in momentary total embarrassment followed by a quick look around to see who saw it. It brings greater attention to all the fundamentals for the next swing. We don't want to repeat it. Naturally, we will receive counsel from our playing partners, such as, you know, "keep your head down."

Leaders also swing and totally miss the ball, which means that their alignment is out of whack. For example, they may develop a plan that totally misses the mark or make a personnel decision that doesn't work out. In golf, the WHIFF may not be observed by one's playing partners, but in leadership it is always noticed. The honest golfer will count the stroke and move on. The real leader accepts the responsibility, learns from the failure, and moves on.

There's another WHIFF that leaders often overlook and one they should pay close attention to in working with others. The spelling is just a little different. It's the WIIFM. Sounds like one of your local FM stations. WIIFM stands for "what's in it for me." This is a question everyone just naturally has on their mind. The leader must recognize and accept this. The question requires an answer for each of those who would follow. The leader who does not pay attention to WIIFMs risks individual and organizational failure. Why? Because when people's interests have not been considered and aligned, their motivation quickly fades. In organizational and team efforts alignment of incentives is critical.

Organizations seek to have employees involved in the work they do and to help in a process of continuous improvement. Those on the front line should have some good sound ideas on what's going right and what's not, and what could be improved. In one example, hourly manufacturing employees were invited to participate in once-a-week brainstorming sessions in an attempt to generate ideas for improving products and processes. All work classifications were represented. Attendance was voluntary.

A tool-and-die journeyman attended the meetings. Now, skilled trades people see themselves as the elite of manufacturing work classifications. In the case of our tool-and-die guy, he manages his own day, his budget, and the schedule for having dies ready when needed. So, he went to the meetings but saw himself as above his nonskilled brothers.

Many of the ideas generated in these meetings required that skilled trades people investigate, test, and develop them. After attending four or five meetings, our tool-and-die guy realized that he was getting assignments, not from management, but from production workers. So, because the meetings were voluntary, he stopped attending to avoid getting extra work for which there was no reward. He had asked the WIIFM question and came up wanting. By not addressing WIIFM questions, management thus lost the participation of people who could most affect change.

Golf is a most competitive sport. You play the course, you play yourself, and you play your opponent. Everything in life's experience exists in golf, and as well in leadership. Both endeavors can be difficult and frustrating. Both offer ultimate challenge and reward. Success at both requires dedication and hard work. Neither relies on strength but rather on timing, feel, coordination, and the desire to get better. You must be prepared to meet challenges in both of these games. The golfer cannot go back to the clubhouse for a club not in the bag to play a shot. Therefore, the golfer needs to be sure the clubs carried are the most effective ones. You, as a leader, are also limited to what is in your bag as you play the leadership game. That's why you need to ensure that you have a comfortable setup—i.e., posture, grip, and alignment—before you do as John Daly is encouraged to do by his golfing galleries, "Grip it, and rip it!"

When you have mastered the fundamentals of golf, you can begin to test your performance by making adjustments that will make you a better player. You may, for example, be able to weaken your grip and hit a Phil Mickleson-like flop shot. You may be able to hit a "draw" or a "fade" to shape your shot to a hole. Move the ball forward or back in your alignment and you'll be able to control the elevation of your shots. You will more and more be able to make the ball do what is needed for the shot.

Mastery of leadership fundamentals sets you up for advancing your skills as a leader. You will be able to maintain your emotional equilibrium because you know what to do and how to do it. You'll be able to play today, tomorrow, and the day after tomorrow. But if you want to play the leadership game to the best of your ability, you've got to develop a "slight edge."

> *I have been able to hope for the best, expect the worst, and take what comes along. If there has been one fundamental reason for my success, this is it.*[6]
>
> Gene Sarazen, one of only a few winners of golf's ''Grand Slam'' (Masters, U.S. Open, British Open, PGA Championship)

Quick Tips for Improving Your Leadership Game

Real leaders typically understand and model the following in their day-to-day actions:

- Leaders deal with the facts. You must judge objectively (factually) while being judged objectively and subjectively, that is, facts, feelings, and perceptions.

- Be politically aware. This doesn't mean "being a politician" or always being politically correct. It means "being realistic" and understanding that many issues have political elements you must comprehend to be successful.

- Building trust is a process. It is not an event. Realize that establishing your associates' trust in you takes time and needs to be continuously safeguarded.

The Slight Edge

Winners listen to other people. They're always trying to learn; they respect other people's opinions. Losers just want to talk.[1]

Doug Sanders, winner of twenty PGA Tour championships

You've played six holes. I hope you found them interesting and reinforcing. Hopefully, you didn't see yourself in too many hazards as you played them. Now, we want to take a look at some holes that will stretch your leadership skills and lead to increased leadership effectiveness. They build on the foundation corners of solid leadership. We see them under the heading, "the slight edge."

Dive Beneath the Surface

In June 2001, a photograph was widely circulated in the press and on the Internet. It was a phenomenal shot of an iceberg found floating off the coast of Newfoundland. Earlier photos of the iceberg had shown only its top extending above the water's surface. It was described as one of the largest icebergs ever seen in the area. Icebergs are obviously a threat to shipping and also to oil-drilling rigs. In fact it is often necessary to divert the path of icebergs away from rigs by towing them with ships.

The iceberg seen floating off Newfoundland came close to a Global Marine Drilling rig. On a beautiful day with the sun directly overhead and the water calm as glass, a diver from the rig went into the water and photographed the entire iceberg.

It is an amazing picture that clearly illustrates the formula that approximately one-third of an iceberg floats above the surface and the other two-thirds are hidden from view. The estimated weight of this particular iceberg was 300,000,000 tons!

You, and many others, resemble the iceberg. You have enormous potential for growth that lies beneath the surface waiting to be released. If you want to be the best leader you can be, you will want to release your presently hidden potential for greater effectiveness.

Are You a Competitor?

Golf is highly competitive. Each year the PGA awards the Vardon Trophy (named for the noted British golfer, Harry Vardon) to the professional player with the lowest stroke average over the tour season. Tiger Woods won the trophy in 2000 with an average of 68.43 strokes per round. Phil Mickleson was second at 69.25, and Ernie Els third with a 69.31 average. So, Woods won by 82/100ths of a stroke over Mickleson, who edged Els by 6/100ths of a stroke. His slight edge earned Woods the Vardon Trophy.

In 1980, the Inverness Club of Toledo, Ohio opened a search for a new golf professional. Among the 280 professionals who submitted applications to Inverness was Don Perne, who indicated on his resume that he was a Master PGA Professional. At the time, Don was one of only two professionals who had been elected to this status. The search committee members asked, "What is a Master PGA Professional?," and the search process was over. Don was hired and served the club in outstanding fashion until his retirement following the Inverness-hosted 1993 PGA Championship. Don's distinction as a Master PGA Professional set him apart from the other applicants for the Inverness job. Today, there are approximately 24,000 PGA club professionals, of which only 250 are designated as Master Professionals. They, like Don Perne, have earned a slight edge.

The 2001 United States Open Championship was played at Southern Hills Country Club in Tulsa, Oklahoma. This annual tournament is open to professional and amateur golfers whose USGA handicap index does not exceed 1.4. The starting field consists of 156 players. The majority of the players (89 in 2001) earn their places through 18-hole local qualifying rounds and 36-hole sectional qualifiers. (A total of 8,398 applications were accepted for the 89 nonexempt slots in the 2001 Open field.) The rest of the players (67 in 2001) are exempt from qualifying on the basis of championships won and/or tournament money earned in the previous year.

All 156 tournament starters play the first and second 18-hole rounds. After 36 holes, the field is cut to the 60 lowest scores and ties. The U.S. Open champion is the player with the lowest score at the end of 72 holes. If there is a tie, it is played off over 18 holes of stroke play on the day following the end of the tournament. If this also results in a tie, the tied players play hole by hole until a winner is decided. Skill and perhaps some good fortune combine to leave only the champion standing.

Golf at the professional level clearly requires a slight edge to finish in a tournament top ten, let alone in first place. Golfers work to develop this slight edge through a dedication to perfecting their skills through countless hours of practice. They know that just a few strokes, often only one or two, are the difference in making a cut, finishing in the top ten, winning, and earning thousands of dollars in prize money. Stories abound of golfers finishing a tournament round and heading directly to the practice range, where they then work until dark trying to achieve the perfection in shot-making they demand of themselves. They fully understand the need to develop a slight edge over their opponents.

One professional is said to end each of his dedicated practice rounds in a unique way. He rings a hole on the practice green with golf balls set about four feet from the cup. When he has successfully putted 100 balls in a row into the cup he quits. Miss one and he starts over!

Course Analysis

Golf commentators on television are mostly ex-professional golfers. They really know the game, the golfers, and the courses played on the various tours. So, it is not surprising that they do an excellent job of analyzing, not only the play of the individual golfers, but the golf courses as well. They tell us which are the easiest holes on the course and why. At the same time they indicate that these are the holes each golfer must play well in order to have a chance at making the cut, because these holes provide the best opportunities for birdies, and even eagles. Play these holes poorly and the odds are that the golfer will be home for the weekend. Play them well and the golfer will probably stay in contention for the tournament lead.

The analysts also point out the holes that offer the most challenge, and therefore the most reward, for those who play them well along with playing the easier ones well. So, the slight edge goes to the combination of playing the easier holes very well, the equivalent of our holes one through six, and adding good play over the more difficult holes, the equivalent of those remaining on our Global Leadership Course.

If you strive to be the best leader you can be, regardless of your position in the organizational hierarchy, developing the slight edge, i.e., being in the upper percentiles of effective leaders, requires dedication and hard work. The development path for excellence in playing the leadership game is no different from the path demanded of the golfer who seeks to be among the best. Your values, adherence to the rules, vision, posture, grip, and alignment give you a leadership foundation. Learning from your leadership experiences provides valuable development opportunities. But it takes sustained extra effort to build the slight edge demonstrated by the best. Let's look at a few examples.

A Slight Edge on the Odds for Survival

Bill Niehous was the general manager of Owens-Illinois Inc.'s Venezuelan operations in the mid-1970s. He was kidnapped by an anti-government radical communist group and was held captive in the jungles of Venezuela for three years. Bill's captivity caused great pain to his family and friends. In most similar circumstances, the captives had been killed by their captors. Bill Niehous lived to tell about his experience following a successful escape attempt.

How did Bill Niehous manage to survive until his eventual return to freedom? Well, I always tell people you would get a good idea if you knew him. Bill speaks Spanish and that certainly was part of his slight edge. Even more, his genuine liking and respect for others, his desire to help and be helpful, a personality that warms you on contact, his ability to be patient and control his emotions, and his great courage in the face of adversity gave him more than a slight edge on the odds for survival. Following his return and later retirement from O-I, Bill Niehous has served a wide variety of community efforts—always in an outstanding fashion. All who know him, admire him. And, he loves the game of golf. We'll hear from Bill when we play hole #17.

On Arrival

A marketing manager recently flew to London via British Airways. The flight was scheduled to land at London's Heathrow Airport. However, due to a labor dispute on the ground the plane was unable to land as scheduled. The flight circled for a time, then was diverted to Stansted Airport where it landed and remained on the runway for a period of time, after which it took off and landed at Heathrow. The delay in Heathrow arrival lasted about 90 minutes. Nothing unusual to this point for those of us experienced in air travel.

However, our marketing manager was impressed. Specifically, she was very surprised how the plane's captain announced the problems of landing at Heathrow. He did not use the standard method of an announcement over the plane's speaker system. Instead, he came into the passenger cabin and made the announcement in person, and in a very personal way, by making his comments in a conversational manner every ten rows or so until he had informed everyone and responded to any questions. And he didn't do this just once, but he repeated the process five times during the ninety-minute delay.

The marketing manager commented, "I could feel the impact of the captain's actions in the plane cabin. People were obviously calmed and put at ease about the situation. He demonstrated his understanding that the passengers deserved both an explanation and his help in adapting to the delay in arriving at their destination. I was impressed by his leadership."

On Departure

After a week in London, our marketing manager was back at Heathrow Airport on a Monday morning to make the return flight to New York. The labor dispute of the previous week had been settled. She arrived at the British Airways counter at 8 A.M. to check-in for her 12:15 P.M. departure. It is always a good practice to allow plenty of time for check-in on international flights. However, she along with others in the processing line were told they would have to wait until 9:30 to be processed. Naturally she thought to herself, "Here we go again."

Yes, but then again, no, as instead of the usual "come back at 9:30, you're on your own till then" there was more to the announcement. There was a surprise for the British Airways customers. All of the waiting passengers were directed to a Quonset hut set up by the airline and asked to go there and relax until 9:30. They were served coffee, tea, and rolls, and provided with comfortable seating. And British Airways people actually asked if there was anything else that might be done to make the wait as enjoyable as possible.

Our marketing manager, reflecting on this experience, said: "I spent three more hours waiting before I was processed. But the British Airways people kept coming around with updates for us and to check that everything was okay. And they were so genuine in the way they did it. Once again, I was really impressed. British Airways, based on my experience, knows what it means to work for a "slight edge" on the competition. They get my vote."

It is not just physical ability or physical characteristics that bring about greatness. In golf, and in leadership, it's about having a passion for the game, being an intense competitor, having a great desire to come out on top, being concerned with what decisions get made, focusing on substance and reality rather than on symbolism and wishful thinking, being willing to work hard, and having the integrity to play by the rules. Greatness comes from within!

What plus How

Today's effective leader must be a "leader of the business" and, even more importantly, a leader of the people. He or she must know what it is that must be accomplished and what needs to be done to ensure successful accomplishment of organizational objectives. The vast majority of leaders understand and aggressively pursue this aspect of leadership, which I call the WHAT. They know WHAT to do. Far too many don't really understand the HOW. They don't know HOW to get it done.

A "leader of the people" knows how to get it done. This is where you want to develop your slight edge. Orchestrate the efforts of your people, utilize and expand their personal capabilities to the fullest, and marry their efforts together to achieve the optimum results. Does this sound like the golfer who knows WHAT is required to play a successful round of golf but must also know HOW to get it done using the tools in his or her golf bag? You bet!

Speaking of tools in the golf bag, my years of experience have taught me that we all have far greater potential for leadership effectiveness than we are exercising. During the balance of the round we're going to play the tools that with use and perfect practice on your part will make you a better leader, even a great leader, to your benefit and that of those whom you serve. The tools include focus, responsibility, confidence, expectations, courage, recognition, feedback, change, help, and optimism.

So You Are Capable—Who Knows It?

Leadership and golf require persistence, dedication, and practice in order to achieve maximum success, i.e. the slight edge. It truly takes more than "who you know" to succeed. Rather, it's "who knows you and your capabilities." Notice the two parts. You must have capabilities and you need to let them shine through to those in position to evaluate your performance. Too often, people do not ensure that their capabilities are known, and therefore they are not brought into play. Play your best clubs, take your best shots. You should not leave knowledge of them to chance. Show the confidence you have in your leadership skills. Ask for, and readily accept, added responsibilities. Your demonstrated leadership performance will win the confidence of others. You will have greater influence in the organization. Your leadership example will rub off on others to their, and the organization's, benefit. In short, step out of the leadership shadows and into the glow of increased leadership success.

Sure, there are exceptions, and some people do advance based on who they know. We love to voice our indignation when this happens. But the truth is that most people get ahead on their merits. They've developed a slight edge in performance. Be objective, take a look around.

Holes 1 through 6 provide a good foundation for anyone interested in playing the leadership game. The remaining holes are designed to challenge you to take advantage of the opportunities available to use your store of potential and develop your personal slight edge and move to the next level in playing the leadership game. Learn to play these holes well. Take their lessons to heart. You will become a more effective leader, you will know it, and so will everyone else. It will be hard work but you'll be a champion at the leadership game.

Remember the advice Jawaharlal Nehru gave to his daughter, Indira Gandhi, who went on to become Prime Minister of India, like her father: "There are two kinds of people, those who do the work and those who take credit for it. Be part of the first group, there are fewer of them."

Leadership is like a race where you run the first few laps as fast as you can and then gradually increase your speed.

FORE! . . . the author

Quick Tips for Improving Your Leadership Game

Real leaders typically understand and model the following in their day-to-day actions:

- SMILE MORE!
- Make it easy for your associates to say, "Have you got a minute?"
- Acquire the habit of thinking and saying "we" rather than "I."

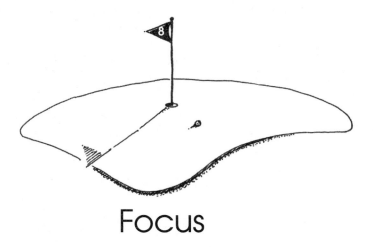

Focus

Tiger Woods at this point in history is rated the number one golfer in the world. He has great natural talent but he has a slight edge on much of his competition. It's his ability to focus.

FORE! . . . the author

All the great golfers, both present and past, share at least one common ability: the ability to focus. They are able to block out what is going on around them and concentrate fully on the shot facing them. When distracted from their focus they do not plunge ahead anyway but rather begin again to set their focus and execute only when they feel right.

In what ranks among the greatest duels in senior golf history, Don Pooley and Tom Watson went head-to-head for 23 holes in the 2002 Senior Open Championship. On the 23rd hole—the 18th hole at Caves Valley Golf Club in Maryland—Pooley had a 10-

foot birdie putt to win. He lined it up, addressed the putt, and then backed away. "My thoughts were going all over the place," Pooley said later, "I had to stop and get refocused." He then made the winning putt.

Vincente Fernandez's caddie helped Fernandez as he prepared to hit a shot from 93 yards out to the pin at the 18th hole during the third round of the 2003 Senior Open Championship. When they were ready, he said to Vincente, simply, "concentrate." Fernandez put the ball within four feet of the pin, sank the putt for a birdie, and finished the day in a tie for second place.

WIN

Golfers focus on each shot. Tiger Woods is so good at this that he can stop a shot in mid-swing, a virtual impossibility for most people. Professional golfers need to hit their best shot(s) in order to win tournaments and/or win as much prize money as possible. They know the importance of focusing on "what's important now," which in acronym form is "WIN."

Golf scores are improved when golfers focus their energy on what they can do, one shot at a time. They do not focus on what they can't do or what other golfers can or cannot do. They concentrate on how they can best improve their opportunity to get the little white ball in the hole in the fewest number of strokes. Golf is a tough game. It is humbling. It is a frustrating game. There are no teammates to pick you up, to take your shot. And there's no place to hide.

Leaders can learn a great deal from watching professional golfers focus in the here and now on the shot immediately facing them. They can also learn from the professional golfer's focus on the future. Professional golfers do not dwell on yesterday's round but learn from it. They focus on today's round in order to shoot the lowest score possible. They think about tomorrow's round in terms of strategy and scoring objectives. And professional golfers focus on the day after tomorrow, i.e., on the opportunity to play in the final two days of a tournament, on the opportunity to play in tournaments of choice, and on maintaining their eligibility to play on the PGA tour. Theirs is a future success orientation.

Leadership in today's competitive organizational life is stressed by demands for innovation. These demands can be so intense that sometimes leaders take their eyes off solid, well-structured, high-value operations. They've been running so well for so long that there is a temptation to pay less attention to them. Leadership takes its eyes off the ball.

A Veritable Cash Cow

For example, a large automobile manufacturing facility had been successfully building and selling a profit-rich luxury model for seven or eight years. Because it was selling so well, and because the initial tooling investment and start-up costs had long since been amortized, the model was a veritable cash cow. Customers were very happy with the product. Dealers continued to serve their repeat customers. Over time there were very few changes to the model. The operation seemed to run itself.

After seven to eight years of marketing bliss, some customer complaints began to surface. The complaints were mostly about nuisance items, such as wind noise, rattles, poorly fitting doors and hoods, and misaligned trim. But management became increasingly concerned: After all this was a luxury model and quality expectations were high.

Attempts to fix the causes of customer concerns focused first on the assembly workers. It was assumed the current workers were not assembling the vehicle correctly. New training programs were devised and presented to the assemblers. But the problems continued to increase. This brought more attention from management, first locally and then from headquarters. Meetings were held, and managers were challenged to ``fix the problem.'' Incentives were implemented. More training was provided to the assemblers.

Still, no improvement. The complaints continued.

Management messages sent to the workers became more strident. Workers needed to be motivated and inspired to build a better vehicle. Posters were put up throughout the plant. Suggestion plan awards were increased. More meetings were held. The problems only got worse. Customer complaints continued in greater numbers. Sales began to waver. Repair costs escalated. Dealers were really upset. More blame was directed at the workers. ``If only the line workers would pay more attention to what they're doing, we wouldn't have these problems.'' Meetings were held with union leaders, who were told the workers needed to do a better job and union leadership could help make this happen.

Finally, top management at headquarters, frustrated with the lack of success, took action. One of the firm's most experienced manufacturing executives was dispatched to spend a day in the assembly plant to see whether he could determine what was going on. He talked with the workers. He walked through every workstation, observed assembly, and asked questions. He rode vehicles through the wind-noise and water-leak tests. He questioned the line supervisors, examined tools, studied the manufacturing process, and read the quality statistics. Then, he once again observed the way the assemblers did their work at each of the line stations, and he talked more with them.

The following morning, at an informal breakfast meeting with several other headquarters executives, he told of his experiences at the plant. ``Yesterday, I had the most interesting experience I've had in my twenty-eight years with the company. I can sum it up in two sentences: Our problem is not that the workers don't know what they are doing. As a matter of fact, they are the reason production is not a lot worse than it is.'' His listeners were astonished as he continued to explain that it was only because of the skill, dedication, and hard work of the assemblers that the vehicles were as good as they were and that there weren't more problems. How could this be?

He continued his observations. "We've been building this model for the past eight years and have considered phasing it out and replacing it with a new model. But sales have remained brisk. The customers have been very loyal. The production costs have long since been amortized and so our profit margins have been excellent. So, we've previously decided not to discontinue the model's production so long as there is a market of satisfied, loyal customers. As this has been happening, the plant's management, and we here at headquarters, have turned our attention away from this operation and not supported the production processes.

"We haven't put a nickel in the operation for years. The tooling is worn out. The machines are out of spec. The dies won't hold to specifications. Sheet metal won't align properly. Doors won't fit. Moldings won't align. The inspection processes have lapsed. Machine maintenance has been reduced and new tools have not been provided. The list is endless. In short, the system that we as management have in place in the operation is incapable of producing the level of quality we want and need. And, it is only the superior effort and skill of the assemblers that is overcoming that lack of capability and making it work at all!"

Leadership Lessons

So, what are the leadership lessons in the foregoing example?

1. Whenever you think a process is working just right, as a leader you need to avoid the temptation to focus all your attention on other issues. Don't take your eye off the ball.

2. Sometimes, even when you think a process is not broke, you should break it. Tiger Woods won the 1997 Masters Championship by 12 strokes with a record score of 270. It is well known that after celebrating his win for a week or so, he looked at videos of his play and determined he had numerous flaws in his swing, particularly in his iron play. He took the next year to overhaul his swing and in another two years, in 2000, played what he calls the "best golf of my life." In his book, *How I Play Golf,* Tiger comments, "I don't know if anyone will ever achieve a state of perfection [with the golf swing], I know I haven't. But you can bet I'll keep trying."[1] Just as the golf swing is always a work in progress, so too the leader should view leadership practices in place as always needing to be in focus. And that is regardless of how good a leader you are, or think you are.

3. Don't waste time blaming the workers or staff when things go wrong. Remember that on hole #6 you were asked to review the first basic principle, which is to "always focus on the situation, issue, problem, decision, or behavior, and not on the person." Spend your time examining the system. Don't ask, "Why can't my people build a good product?" Ask, "What is it about the system that produces defective products?" School critics are fond of asking, "Why can't Johnny read?" when they should be asking, "What is it about our program to teach reading that produces students who can't read?" Remember, managers work IN the system, leaders work ON the system.

4. Who has the greatest effect on the performance of a ship at sea? The captain? The navigator? The chief engineer? Well, it's none of the above. It is the ship's designer who affects the ship's performance more than anyone else. Leaders are designers. Think of them as golf club designers. They need to concentrate on providing the best tools, systems, and processes for achieving objectives, whether on the golf course or in the organizational environment. Their focus should be on continuing success and making change before change is made necessary by someone who has had their eye on the future

Just the Facts

Leaders and golfers need to be able to focus their attention on the situation or issue confronting them. In addition, leaders need to focus on behavior and not on the person(s). Leaders must deal with the facts and not with their feelings. They should know the feelings of others, for these are facts, but must set aside their own feelings as not being factual but subjective data. So, simply stated, it is a fundamental principle that leaders focus on the situation, issue, or behavior and not on the person. As Sergeant Joe Friday of *Dragnet* fame would say, "Just give me the facts, ma'am, just the facts."

In life, we as individuals are quite limited in what we are able to personally control. If we are strict about the definition of control, we find the only thing we can really control is our own behavior. The golfer in playing a round of golf is affected by a variety of elements over which he or she has no control. This can be frustrating.

Albert

I was introduced to Albert, an inveterate golfer, about fifteen years ago. The introduction occurred one morning as we were about to begin a leadership session. One of the participants, recently returned from an overseas assignment in England, handed me an advertisement he had torn out of a magazine. It was a full page ad for "Glenmuir Sportswear of Lanark, Scotland, Telephone 0555 2241." Readers were asked to "Visit your local pro shop and ask for Glenmuir golfwear. Our high quality pullovers, intarsias, and cardigans are made from 100 percent pure double lambswool. Pullovers, shirts, and jackets are available in a wide range of fashionable colours." This was the only reference to Glenmuir on the page. The rest of the page was devoted to the tale of "Albert's Ashes."

Albert was ninety-five years old and had played golf for eighty years. He loved his golf, and he never played without his Glenmuir cashmere pullover. [Oops—forgot this crass commercial reference.] Albert's only regret during his long playing career was that he had never holed out on the 18th green.

He would play his drive into the river that crossed the fairway, or lose his ball in the severe rough on the left. Sometimes, already beaten, he would pick up before his final putt.

The opening day of the season arrived and Albert was playing inspired golf. He had played 17 holes in par and had now put his second shot on the 18th within six inches of the pin.

Albert withdrew his putter, lined it up, took his stance, and died of a heart attack. After the cremation, his widow explained to the vicar that she would like Albert's ashes to be placed in the hole on the 18th green.

At last Albert's time had come. Every member turned out to see his widow perform the ceremony. She knelt down by the hole, closed her eyes, tipped the urn . . . and the wind blew Albert out of bounds.

As Albert knew from his life and death experiences on his club's 18th hole, there was much that was outside his own sphere of control (see Figure 8-1). In fact, in the strict sense of control, Albert, like the rest of us, controlled only his own behavior. And sometimes we are better at doing it than at other times. Witness the behavior of golfers such as "Terrible Tommy" Bolt, John Daly's past behavior on not-so-good holes or days, or Kevin Costner's character in the movie *Tin Cup*. The golfer pays a price when he or she loses control, so does the leader. And they have only themselves to blame.

The Spheres of Influence

Outside the sphere of control, as shown in Figure 8-1, is the sphere of influence. The golfer attempts to exercise influence over the environment by taking into account such things as the lie of the ball, distance to the hole, wind, natural impediments, the caddy's advice, and so on. The leader influences outcomes through

FIGURE 8-1.
Spheres of influence.

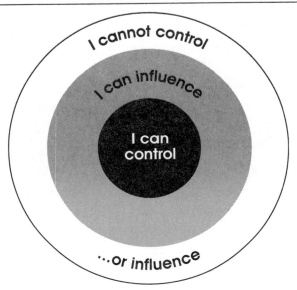

What can you control?

What can you influence?

What can't you control or influence?

associates, peers, the boss, spouse, clients, or groups. The size of this sphere is dependent on a person's skills as leader and communicator and it can expand in proportion to how well these skills are exercised. This is the portion of the sphere of influence that offers the greatest opportunity for leadership growth.

Influence is exercised by asking questions: "What are you going to do?" "What can I do to help?" "How should we proceed?" No matter how these questions are answered they will help to focus on the situation, issue, or behavior that is being acted upon. They will flush out whether in fact there is opportunity to exercise some influence.

It is critical to a golfer's success to maintain focus on those elements of the game that their behavior can control or influence. The same applies to the leader playing the leadership game. One of the major causes of stress for leaders is not focusing their actions appropriately because they fail to recognize what they need to control and what they can only influence.

I entered the Navy as an ensign commissioned through the NROTC program at Marquette University. As a midshipman, I received some training and indoctrination, but simply stated, I was the stereotypical "bull ensign" reporting to active duty. However, I had a coach, my older brother, Ray, who had survived the European Theatre in World War II. He advised me to seek the help of the leading enlisted person assigned to the shipboard division for which I was given responsibility. *Thanks Coach Ray!*

I reported aboard the USS Lincoln County (LST 898) on an August evening in Yokosuka, Japan. The next morning I went to Chief's quarters and introduced myself to Chief Quartermaster Dominic Bruni. Notice, I did not ask the Chief to come to Officer's Country, but rather went to his home turf. During our conversation, I explained to the Chief that I really didn't know much about electronics or many of the other aspects of our divisional (operations) responsibilities. This was, of course, no surprise to the Chief! We wound up our conversation with my request for the Chief's "help" in learning my job responsibilities and in being able to lead the division so that we could perform as effectively as possible. His response was a sincere, "Yes, sir," and Chief Bruni lived up to that commitment. He was my first caddie and at the time I'd yet to play my first round of golf. *Never forget Chief Bruni!*

I had another lifelong learning experience about eighteen months later. I was still serving aboard the USS Lincoln County in the not-so-glamorous "Gator Navy," which was the amphibious ships and equipment dedicated to supporting troop movements and amphibious landings. I was within six months of release from active duty or transfer to another command. Our new commanding officer thought it would be a good idea to move his officers around and have them gain experience in other assignments. This is an excellent concept, as I have learned over the years, but at the time I didn't think so. After all, I was comfortable in my billet. Control and influence were in good balance.

Well, my new assignment was to be the First Lieutenant. The responsibilities included all the above-deck evolutions of the ship, such as anchoring, mooring, loading and off-loading materials and equipment, servicing and manning our two anti-aircraft batteries, maintenance and painting, and so on. None of this fell within either my skill or interest level. Consequently, though the Captain said "here's what you're going to do" and I said "aye, aye, sir," my mind was saying "I really don't want to do this!" I know many of you have had this kind of experience.

The fight was on between what I physically had to do and what I mentally didn't want to do. I wanted to control the situation and not do what I'd been assigned to do. This I call self-inflicted stress, and it causes both mental and physical distress. I began to experience both. As I struggled, I was helped by my wife Ann, who had her own hands full with a baby, Mark, and who was pregnant with Tim. She didn't need another "baby" on her hands!

Fortunately, we remembered the lesson learned eighteen months before, which I'd forgotten at the time but have remembered ever since. It was my brother's advice. Acknowledge what you know and, more importantly, what you don't know, and get the help needed. So, once again I made a special trip to Chief's quarters. This time it was to see Chief Gunner's Mate Warren Brickey, who was the leading petty officer for my newly assigned Deck Division. We struck the same deal that Chief Bruni and I had agreed upon eighteen months before. Once again reality was recognized. Control and influence were properly assigned, and life was great. *Never forget Chief Brickey!*

I feel very fortunate to have learned at an early adult age the following lesson, which I've tried to practice. Those who know me best have heard me offer it to them, probably too many times. But it is so valuable. "Remember, control yourself the best you can, try to exert as much influence as possible to make the right things happen, and don't spend your time thinking and worrying about that which you cannot control and/or influence." You'll be more productive and as a bonus you will sleep better each night!

The golfer knows that once the club has been swung, the contact with, flight, bounce, and roll of the ball is out of his or her control and influence. The effective leader knows that you can lead by example. You can influence others by communicating your expectations. You can work to establish a motivational environment. However, only they can control their behavior. The belief that you can control the behavior of others, including those you lead, brings stress and self-doubt when you fail to do so.

It is possible to become so focused on all the things you cannot control and/or influence that you lose sight of what you are in fact capable of doing. When that happens you can create a lot of unhealthy anxiety and frustration for yourself. For golfers, their scores go up and their ability to compete at an acceptable level is threatened. For leaders, it blurs the realistic sphere of control and influence and will probably result in a drop in performance.

Tiger Woods may be a brilliant performer on the golf course, yet Tiger is also human. The game is golf. You, the leader, are human. The game is leadership. On the golf course and in leadership, perfection is a myth. You can make a positive difference, however, and you can approach excellence if you maintain a focus on what you can realistically accomplish and conscientiously and courageously pursue that focus. The golfer decides which club can best control the shot required, selects the club that can best influence the desired result, focuses, and executes the shot. The leader's execution needs to be no less focused.

Here are a few suggestions to help you focus:

- Control your time.
- Avoid distractions that take you away from your priorities.
- Control your emotions.
- Question every meeting invitation.
- Don't over-react when things go badly.
- Maintain your self-confidence.

- Give yourself time to think.
- "Close the door."
- Buy another wastebasket!

I'm playing great, for me, and then I just lose my focus.

Ken Smith, fellow duffer

Quick Tips for Improving Your Leadership Game

Real leaders typically understand and model the following in their day-to-day actions:

- Life will be much simpler and far less stressful if you focus on and work within your "sphere of influence."
- Direct your energies to achieving short-term goals and objectives but never lose sight of the ultimate purpose (vision) you are pursuing.
- Maintain a constancy of purpose. Avoid the "program of the day" syndrome.
- Help others succeed.

Responsibility

The price of greatness is responsibility.

Winston Churchill

The Masters Tournament is held annually at the Augusta National Golf Club in Augusta, Georgia. The score sheets for the tournament carry a message from its founder, the golfing great Bobby Jones. "In golf, customs of etiquette and decorum are just as important as rules governing play." Spectators and golfers alike are reminded of their responsibilities.

In addition to following the rules of golf as they play, golfers have other responsibilities. They essentially boil down to "keeping their house (course)" in order. For example, divots (turf removed by the club during a shot) are to be replaced, sand traps are to be raked following recovery from the misfortune of having landed in one, golf carts and golf bags are never to be placed on the green, and players behind you are not to be held up unnecessarily.

Peter Koestenbaum in his book, *Leadership: The Inner Side Of Greatness*, states that leading requires "ownership" of the meanings of personal responsibility and accountability. According to Christine Brennan:

> Now, more than ever, I am convinced our national pastime should be golf. . . . There is no game on the sports landscape more noble and pure than golf. It's the only sport I know in which the players at all levels, from beginner to millionaire, willingly call penalties on themselves.[1]

Pay for Responsible Play

So, golf is an honorable game, a responsible game, a game in which the majority of players, being honorable, responsible people, don't need referees or umpires. On the Golf Channel, no one blames America for everything bad that happens to them. In golf, you alone are ultimately responsible for what happens to you. No whining is allowed on the Golf Channel. Your ball ended up where it did because you hit it there or because it took a crazy, uncontrollable bounce. Too bad, that's golf . . . that's life . . . that's leadership.

Professional golfers are compensated in direct proportion to how well they play. They don't hold out for more money, or demand new contracts, because of someone else's deal. When they make a mistake, no one is there to cover for them or back them up. Golfers cannot fail 70 percent of the time, like .300 hitters in baseball, and expect to make $10 million a season.

During the economic boom years of the 1990s, there was little complaint regarding executive compensation. However, behavior that was once acceptable, or simply overlooked, can overnight be seen as outrageous and irresponsible. Institutional investors and shareholders express their unhappiness with large executive compensation plans and poor corporate performance. The value of many large companies has been significantly reduced and in some cases virtually wiped out. Yet, the pay of their leaders has risen, their pensions have been protected while those of many long-service employees have been reduced severely, and golden parachutes are still there if they are forced to leave their organizations. They seem to be rewarded for just being there. This doesn't just occur in business. It's happening in health care, government, and, critics would say, most egregiously in higher education. If these so-called leaders were golfers, they wouldn't make the cut and they wouldn't be paid.

Golf is an honorable game. Its rules do not change. Leadership too is an honorable game. Its rules also do not change. Your school may have done away with winners and losers but golf has not. Your school may have abolished failing grades, now giving "students" as many chances as they need to get the right answer, or credit just for "trying" even if they never get it right! This doesn't bear the slightest resemblance to anything in real life.

Golf is the model for real life. In real life people actually have to play their own ball. Real leaders play their own ball. It's their responsibility. And they insist others play responsibly as well.

Top Finishers Are the Best Prepared

An unknown author wrote, "Success has a thousand fathers. Failure is an orphan." Some golfers may seek to blame their poor play on the environment (wet grounds, too much wind, old clubs, or pin placements). The dedicated golfer attempts to improve the ability to play well no matter the conditions. Whether greens are wet or dry, slow or fast, they've practiced how to play them. The conditions of play are not always the same for golfers in competition. If you have witnessed the variances in weather from morning to afternoon in British Open play you know what I mean. The top finishers are the players best prepared to handle the contingencies. They've developed the needed skills through responsible preparation. Long hours of practice in all kinds of conditions may not be fun but they do it because it is necessary to increase their skills to gain the "slight edge." They assume the responsibility for improved effectiveness. They want to win but know winning is not easy. This is true of responsible leaders as well.

Committed leaders will assume more responsibilities than they are formally assigned in order to accomplish goals they believe in. They will accept less than ideal working conditions, make do with fewer resources than they would like, and even work with little or no appreciation from the boss as long as they can be successful. If the leader acts responsibly, he or she can inspire others to succeed. In doing so , the organization, the team, and the leader are well served. As in golf, this kind of a win is never along the path of least resistance.

According to Koestenbaum, the leadership mind is characterized by "hope", i.e., by the realistic perception that there is a way out, that there is a future, that there is a solution. This is the golfer who must put an errant shot, a bad hole, or a bad round out of his or her mind and focus on doing well on the next hole or in the next round. This is the leader who lives not only in yesterday and today as administrators do, not only in yesterday, today, and tomorrow as managers do, but who lives in yesterday, today, tomorrow, and most importantly in the day after tomorrow.

What Matters Most

Philosophy is the world's oldest science. Today's proliferating leadership techniques (panaceas) are adjuncts to the tradition of leadership philosophy. They may be helpful in a technical, by-the-numbers sense, but they are not effective substitutes for the depth of a philosophy. Leadership philosophy is the seat of self, the foundation of the soul, the leadership character. Character means depth, not technique. Integrity means substance, not form. In our leadership affairs, we must allow our consciences to call us back to the things that matter most. Leading requires "ownership" of the meanings of personal responsibility and accountability. Leadership is an honorable game.

Oops!

A number of years ago an incoming jumbo jet from the Far East landed short of the runway at San Francisco International Airport. Unfortunately, as those of you who have flown into San Francisco know, this meant the plane landed in San Francisco Bay. At the inquiry into what had happened to cause this crash landing, the pilot was asked for his explanation. To the great surprise of all in attendance at the hearing he responded, "I screwed up."

A Case of Corporate Responsibility

In the Fall of 1982, Johnson & Johnson was confronted with a crisis when seven people in Chicago died mysteriously. It was determined that each of the people who had died had ingested an Extra-Strength Tylenol capsule laced with cyanide. The news caused an immediate nationwide panic.

Johnson & Johnson's response was unusual for a corporation in crisis. In other similar cases, companies put themselves first. For example, when benzene was found in Source Perrier's bottled water, instead of accepting accountability, they claimed it was only an isolated incident and recalled a limited amount of product in North America. When the benzene was later found in their bottled water in Europe, they had to issue a worldwide recall. Consumers around the world had apparently been drinking contaminated water for months. Source Perrier was widely criticized for lack of responsibility and disregard for public safety.

Johnson & Johnson's responsible actions in dealing with the Tylenol crisis led also to the product's comeback in the marketplace. Chairman James E. Burke said, "It will take time, it will take money, and it will be very difficult; but we consider it a moral imperative, as well as good business, to restore Tylenol to its position [as the number one alternative to aspirin as an over-the-counter pain killer]."[2]

The universal human response to a failed situation or "screwup" is to find someone or something else to blame, or to give a rationalizing justification for the unsatisfactory turn of events. This is the well-known phenomenon known as CYA (cover your posterior). We see the difference between a responsible leadership approach and CYA in the actions of Johnson & Johnson and Source Perrier.

Mountain Dew: A Case of Individual Responsibility

A huge NATO naval exercise was conducted in the Pacific Ocean. The exercise lasted forty-five days. Ship replenishment was a major responsibility of both ship and shore participants. Among the orders placed with a shore supply facility was one for $3,000 worth of Mountain Dew soda, approximately 1,500 12-packs. As you probably know, Mountain Dew contains caffeine and is a favorite of night-watch-standing Navy personnel. The order was intended to supply several ships in addition to the one that was picking it up at the shore facility.

The receiving ship's supply officer, a lieutenant commander, was supervising the loading of replenishments, when he was joined on the pier by the shore facility's supply officer, a lieutenant.

The lieutenant commander said, "Everything is going well except I don't see our Mountain Dew anywhere."

The lieutenant said, "I'll check on it," and went directly to his leading petty officer, who was supervising the operation on the pier. He quickly learned there was no Mountain Dew on the pier for loading and no paperwork indicating it had been ordered. He reported this to the lieutenant commander.

"I know we ordered it," responded the lieutenant commander in a concerned but not offensive manner. So, the lieutenant went back to his offices to check, and, wouldn't you know, he found the order on his desk, buried under a pile of papers. He had obviously missed it. He knew he was at fault and immediately reported the mistake to his boss, the chief of staff for supply, who commented, "You screwed up, but it's not mission critical. Go tell them what happened."

The lieutenant hustled back down to the pier and advised the lieutenant commander of his error. Though he was upset, the lieutenant commander accepted the lieutenant's apology. They agreed the Mountain Dew would be on the pier the following week when the replenishment ship returned, and the shore facility would bear the cost of $3,000.

A simple story but with great leadership impact. The lieutenant recognized he had made a mistake and took immediate responsibility for it. Both the lieutenant commander and the chief of staff acted responsibly in accepting the lieutenant's explanation and apology, took into account the otherwise excellent job he and his people were doing under the stressful activity of the fleet exercise, and kept their cool.

The reaction of the chief of staff left the lieutenant with the feeling that he could ``go to the boss'' with anything and would not be blown out of the water without a fair hearing. The incident, handled responsibly by all involved, set the stage for a continuing open relationship regarding the sharing of positive, and not so positive, communications.

A Case of Irresponsibility

A local supplier was receiving complaints from a customer that a plastic part was not fitting properly under a fender during vehicle assembly operations and was causing production problems. So, a two-person team, consisting of a management and a union representative, went to the customer's plant to see whether they could determine the cause of the problem. As they observed the operation, they noticed that the woman who was putting the part on the left fender was having a very difficult time while the man assembling on the right fender had no problems at all. They watched the operation with the supervisor for about twenty minutes and were just about ready to leave the line when the supervisor was called away. They watched the two assemblers for another moment or two and then the male assembler left his station and approached them.

``Do you recognize what's just happened to you?'', he asked.

They shook their heads, not knowing what the fellow was driving at.

``I usually work the side you've been watching,'' he said, ``and I don't have any problems at all. Mary has never done the job before. She was placed there a half hour ago with no training, just before you got here. The foreman thinks the production rates are too high so he figures out ways to slow things down and blames the lower production on the parts not fitting.''

The team tried, and others from the supplier did as well, to convince the customer that the parts were fine but couldn't do anything about the supervisor's sabotage of the process. The problem lasted two years. It was resolved when the supervisor was transferred.

Someone Needs to Step Up

A multi-location home products company initiated a comprehensive employee involvement program. A major aspect of the program was the solicitation of ideas from employees. The idea for a fitness center was presented for review by a steering committee. The committee was made up of four hourly and four salaried employees. The proposal suggested that due to space limitations it would be necessary to build a second floor over part of the existing company building at the cost of about $400,000. This did not include the exercise equipment. The total cost including equipment would be $600,000.

The pressure to make employee involvement work was intensely felt throughout the organization. So, although the steering committee members all felt that the idea was far too expensive, no one would stand up and say, ``No, we can't do this.''

And, in the age-old tradition of not biting the responsibility bullet, the steering committee recommended the presentation for the fitness center be given to the divisional steering committee. It was, and you guessed it, from there it was passed on to corporate because no one would say, ``No, this shouldn't be done. There are cost problems, space problems, what about insurance, who's going to monitor the center, etc.''

The fitness center was built. Now the company has a fitness center at each of its fifty or so locations. Maybe this was a good idea right from the start. I don't know. But the process is familiar and it is not a responsible one. It reminds me of an illustration I often use. The leader is walking along this dock toward the water, which is thirty feet deep off the end of the dock. Followers line the dock. You, the leader, can't swim. Do you want your people cheering "Go for it!" Or, do you want them yelling, "Stop, you'll drown!" I know what my preference is, what's yours?

Lose Responsibility, Lose Control

Few people stop to realize that in blaming others or escaping responsibility through justification, one is at the same time losing control of the situation. (It is equivalent to the golfer blaming the club, the caddie, or the weather. The stroke, the score, still stands.) The individual who accepts 100 percent responsibility for all events and relationships in which he or she takes part is thereby empowered. External events (the club, the caddie, the weather) do indeed add an uncontrollable factor, but if the individual acts as if 100 percent responsible, then there is no possibility of evasion through blame or justification. The result is that the individual is forced to examine ways to improve the situation

Evasion is basically passive; its opposite is the active role, which provides the person who accepts responsibility with an effective response to the screw-up. This holds true for work-related tasks and for personal relationships. A responsible person looks into all options, examines them, and is empowered to direct the situation by choosing one. The individual is strengthened, the fear of embarrassment or ridicule is minimized, and most importantly, the situation moves positively toward improved results.

Why Are You Sawing that Hole?

A group of people were on a sightseeing boat touring the San Diego harbor. A woman observed a man seated in a chair. She couldn't believe what she was seeing. He had a saw and was sawing a hole in the bottom of the boat right where he sat! "Stop that," she yelled, "what do you think you're doing? You'll sink the boat!"

"Lady," he replied, "this is my seat, and I'll do with it what I want."

Responsibility is not doing what you want to do, especially at the risk of harming others. It is not rank or privilege. It is doing the right thing and expecting no less from others.

The real golfer, playing the honorable game of golf, accepts 100 percent responsibility and moves forward. The real leader, playing the honorable game of leadership, can and should do no less!

FORE! . . . the author

Quick Tips for Improving Your Leadership Game

Real leaders typically understand and model the following in their day-to-day actions:

- Believe that you have the power to make a difference and take responsibility for trying to make that difference.
- Be a fixer, not a finger-pointer.
- View the failure of an associate to succeed as your failure unless you have done everything possible to enable the associate's success.
- If one of your associates has a chronic performance problem that no one has addressed, then you deal with it.

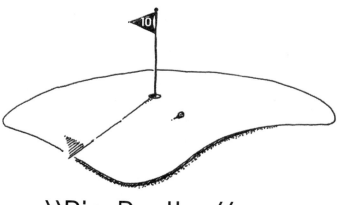

"Big Bertha": Confidence

Initiated by Muhammad Ali's perpetual boasts of "I am the greatest," a colleague asked the boxer what he was like at golf. "I'm the best," replied Ali, "I just haven't played yet."

Little Brown Book of Anecdotes

I was listening to ESPN Radio one morning. The conversation topic was, "What is the hardest sport?" The consensus selection seemed to be golf. Surprising, yes, but think about it. Golf can be considered the hardest sport at which to become competitive, and then remain competitive. Why? Well, it's all in the swing.

Ask any golfer, "Is it easy to develop an effective golf swing?" The answer will probably be something like, "Sure, I can show you how to stand, grip the club, and swing so you make contact with the ball.'' Change the question to, "How hard is it to develop a golf swing that will consistently result in my hitting the golf ball the desired distance and in the direction selected?"

The answer will be something like, "Only the pros can do that and even they have difficulty at times." You've heard the saying, so and so seems like a "lost soul." It well describes the golfer who loses his or her golf swing. They don't know what to do. The swing is critical to success. Golfers have lost their swing and have found it. Some have lost it and reconstructed it. Others have lost it and never been able to regain the desired consistency of distance and direction. Losing the ability to swing the golf club effectively is painful to the amateur. It is career threatening to the professional.

At this writing, David Duval, who only a few years ago was contesting Tiger Woods for the number one world ranking among professional golfers, is struggling with his swing. Duval won the British Open Championship in 2001. His best finish in 2003 was a tie for 28th place at the FBR Capital Open and he was ranked 98th in the world. Duval shot an 80 in the opening round of the 2003 PGA Championship and missed the cut. He has also suffered, and seemingly overcame, back and wrist injuries. Back, wrist, and shoulder injuries are quite common among golfers. Here again it's the swing. Hopefully, as you read this, David Duval has once again put his name on the leader board.

Yips!

Ian Baker Finch won the 1991 British Open and shortly thereafter quit playing professional golf. As the story goes, Finch could not overcome the putting "yips." This term is used to describe a sudden twitching that can cause even the best golfer to miss a putt from only inches away. Finch is now a very successful and effective golf commentator on ABC Television.

A former colleague of mine at Owens-Illinois Inc., Russ Berkoben, is a one-handicap golfer. He has won many amateur tournaments in Ohio. Russ admits to occasionally suffering from the "yips." So, he did not pass up a recent opportunity to participate in a study of this putting affliction conducted by the Mayo Clinic! Now this must be serious stuff!

Whether the golfer's swing is affected by injury, the "yips," or other influences, its effectiveness is critical to golfing success. The golfer must be able to play with confidence, a confidence in his or her golf swing. The game of golf requires precise physical movement and a relaxed, confident mental state. Disrupt the physical mechanics and the mental state suffers as well. The result is a golfer who lacks confidence. No equipment change will cure this condition.

Once Upon a Name

There are many everyday words that have evolved from people's names. They are called "eponyms," which comes from the Greek word meaning "upon a name." But, of course you knew that. Here's an eponym for you: Bertha.

In 1902 at the age of 16, Bertha Krupp inherited her family's Krupp weapons works, Germany's leading manufacturer of munitions since the eighteenth century. During World War I, Bertha's firm designed and manufactured a gigantic 94-ton mortar. This howitzer had a muzzle a foot-and-a-half wide. The British nicknamed it, "Big Bertha." Golfers know the rest of story.

The Calloway "Big Bertha" was among the first, if not the first, of the over-sized drivers now popular in golf, especially among amateur golfers. The over-sized heads on these clubs are now so large they virtually eliminate "whiffs," and they are designed to provide even more distance than their predecessors. They are designed to mechanically improve the golfer's ability to drive the golf ball. But overall improvement in one's golf game requires much more. Big Bertha truly helps only those who swing it with the confidence that they will achieve greater distance, together with desired direction, of ball flight.

Julie

A good friend, let's call her Julie, describes her golf life as having started in 1989, when she played regularly in a company-sponsored league and on Saturday mornings with three friends. Julie describes her play as adequate. In 1994, her work schedule conflicted with golf, so she quit playing. In 2001, after not having touched a club for seven years, Julie once again was talked into playing in a company league. In her words, "I was so bad, it wasn't any fun at all. I don't like to do things poorly. I quit golf and I'm not going to play it any more." Julie has no confidence in her ability to ever play the game.

Jim's 5-Iron

Three former colleagues of mine were conducting training at General Motors' then Central Foundry Division in Saginaw, Michigan. They were all invited to play in the division's annual golf outing. The colleague who told me the story, Chuck, said he luckily had a fairly new set of clubs, which he would not be embarrassed to be seen playing with. He, and his boss Dick, both came with full sets of clubs ready to play. The third member of the group, Jim, showed up as well. However, all he was carrying was a single club, a 5-iron. He used it off the tee, on the fairway, and on the greens. He drew a lot of stares. At the end of the day, Dick had shot a 91, Chuck had a 107, and Jim shot 88. Chuck said, "I was ready to throw away all my clubs but my 5-iron." Jim had confidence in his ability to play one club, the 5-iron, and so he played it.

Start Slow/Bounce Back

Our son, Kevin, whom you met earlier on the practice tee, played in a U.S. Junior national qualifier meet at the Muirfield Memorial Course in Dublin, Ohio. This is the site of the annual Jack Nicklaus-sponsored Memorial Tournament. The junior tournament was for players age 18 and under who had met a qualifying handicap. There were over 220 participants. They played from the back, or professional, tees. Spectators, mostly relatives and friends, surrounded the first tee and watched as the young players started their rounds. Kevin, to his embarrassment, topped his tee shot. It went 30 or 40 yards. He proceeded to score a double-bogey 6 on the par-4 hole. Then he made a triple-bogey 8 on the par-5 second hole, and another double-bogey 6 on the par-4 third hole. After three holes, he was seven shots over par on the par-72 course. He then proceeded to par the next 15 holes. He finished with a 79, which placed him third in the field of over 220 golfers. Kevin didn't quit. He kept his confidence, and in golfing parlance was able to "bounce back."

Tough Question

In the late 1980s and early 1990s, I helped facilitate the previously mentioned Leadership NOW activity for General Motors Corporation. During this time I was privileged to work with over 800 GM leaders in forty groups over a four-year period. Many of my former colleagues were participants in the activity.

Early in each of the five-day program sessions, I asked these organizational leaders to identify the characteristics of effective leaders. Invariably one characteristic was not mentioned. Even when I offered the hint, "it begins with C," it was not named until the fifth or sixth guess. The characteristic is "confidence," which is the belief in one's own abilities. I have continued to ask groups of leaders to identify the characteristics of leadership and, unfortunately, with the same result regarding confidence.

How's Your Confidence?

Lack of confidence in one's ability to lead may be the single greatest failing of the modern manager. Leaders, like golfers, must be confident in their ability to play the game. If you do not have any confidence in your ability to lead, as Julie didn't with the game of golf, you should not be in the leadership game. Don't get into it for money or status. If you don't have confidence in your ability to succeed, you will fail. You can't compete in the leadership game over time with only one club, as Jim did with relative success compared to Dick and Chuck. Those who can play their full set of clubs effectively will outscore you. You will need confidence in your ability to lead and a full set of leadership competencies to be most successful.

You will also need what Kevin demonstrated, the ability to retain your confidence in the face of adversity and to not quit. You will need to be able to "bounce back." You don't need to have the "most confidence" vis-à-vis all other professional golfers, which Paul Azinger attributed to Tiger Woods on ESPN-TV on June 16, 2001, after Tiger had come back from nine shots off the lead at the 2001 U.S. Open. But it is a worthy goal.

In his book *How I play Golf*, written with the Editors of *Golf Digest*, Tiger Woods describes confidence in the following way. "Confidence is easier to define than it is to measure. It is an assuredness in one's ability to accomplish a task even under the most stressful circumstances. Success breeds confidence."[1] Champions and real leaders are confident people. They can survive the natural ups and downs of golf, leadership, and life itself. How would you rate your leadership confidence?

How Do They Do It?

You can't make up for a lack of confidence with a "bigger Big Bertha!" You need to do what Bruce Lietzke was apparently able to do as a teenager learning to play the game of golf. Beginning in the early 1980s, and until he joined the PGA's Champions Tour, Lietzke had the reputation of being the golfer who didn't practice. He played only those tournaments that did not conflict with other interests, particularly family priorities. Yet he won thirteen tournaments on the PGA Tour and enjoyed a healthy income. He has also performed impressively as a senior golfer, including winning the 2003 Senior Open. How has Lietzke done it?

Bruce Lietzke has what we all have to a greater or lesser degree, which is muscle memory. He is able to swing a golf club a few times and the muscles respond to his long established swing pattern. This ability can also be described as unconscious competence. Figure 10-1 illustrates the competence development process.

Just as Bruce Lietzke and other highly capable golfers develop

FIGURE 10-1.
Levels of competency.

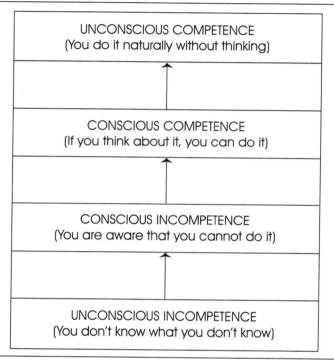

UNCONSCIOUS COMPETENCE
(You do it naturally without thinking)

CONSCIOUS COMPETENCE
(If you think about it, you can do it)

CONSCIOUS INCOMPETENCE
(You are aware that you cannot do it)

UNCONSCIOUS INCOMPETENCE
(You don't know what you don't know)

unconscious competence in their golf swings, so too do leaders need to develop an unconscious competence regarding leadership fundamentals and play accordingly. Confidence will then flow from this competence. The competence will come more easily to some than to others, just as with the golf swing, but you can do it if you work at it.

Divots

Competence builds confidence. Chris Riley, a PGA Tour player, was playing the final round of the 2003 Greater Hartford Open when his last tee shot of the day came to rest in a fairway divot, essentially a hole left when an earlier shot lifted the turf from the fairway. Hitting out of the divot can be tricky. While our "Tuesday Group" members would have moved the ball onto fairway grass, the professional must play it where it lies. Consequently, Riley had to play out of the divot, just as he would have to play his ball if it were behind a tree (in the 2003 Buick Open, Tiger Woods hit a ball under a tree from a kneeling position), or if it were buried in a sand bunker. Now, Riley has prepared himself through practice to competently hit his ball out of a divot. Among his action choices, individually or in combination, are to move the ball back in his stance (trap it sooner), use a more lofted club (the ball will come out low and hot), and/or make a descending angle toward the ball (pop it out). So, he approaches the shot with confidence. Riley swings, the ball leaves the divot, and the ball lands on the green finishing about 12 feet from the hole. Riley calmly rolls in a birdie putt.

Leaders must play a lot of decisions from divots, behind trees, and out of sand traps. It's the nature of the leadership game. It is why effective leaders are paid so handsomely. After all, if there were no hazards to overcome in running effective organizations there would be no need for leaders. The only answer to hazards is competence and confidence. Golf shots do not always drop in the hole. Leadership actions and decisions are not always successful, but your odds of success go way up with competence and confidence.

What's Your Bounce Back Percentage?

I introduced the notion of "bounce back" earlier. The PGA Tour compiles over thirty individual statistics on each PGA professional, including, for example, driving distance, number of putts per round, and scoring average.

One such statistic is the "bounce back percentage," which is the percent of time that a player is over par on a hole and then is under par on the following hole. Essentially it measures a player's ability to rebound from a poor performance on a particular hole. Is he physically and mentally able to put the poor score, poor swing, poor putt, or bad break of the previous hole behind him?

As of this writing, the number one and number two ranked players in the world, Tiger Woods and Ernie Els, are tied at 29 percent for the top spot in this particular category. Sports psychologist Dr. Bob Rotella says, "One of the ironies of golf is that bad players have a harder time accepting bad shots than good players do."[2] If you want to raise your bounce back percentage, work on your leadership competencies. Increased confidence will follow.

A Helping Hand

An octogenarian, who was an avid golfer, moved to a new town and joined the local golf club. He went to the club for the first time to play but was told there wasn't anyone with whom he could play. He was pretty insistent that he wanted to play. Finally, the assistant professional said he would play with him and asked how many strokes he wanted for a bet.

The 80-year old said, "I really don't need any strokes because I've been playing quite well. The only real problem I have is getting out of sand traps."

And he did play well. Coming to the 18th hole, they were all even. The pro had a nice drive, was on the green in two, and two-putted for a par. The old man had a nice drive too, but his second shot went into a sand trap next to the green. He blasted out of the sand, his ball landed on the green, and then rolled into the hole. Birdie, match, and the money!

The pro walked over to the sand trap where his opponent still stood. He looked down and said, "Nice shot, but I thought you said you have a problem getting out of sand traps?"

"I do," replied the octogenarian, "would you please give me a hand?"

Three Wonderful Examples

Competence and confidence, along with the acknowledgment of one's weaknesses, can come with age, as was the case with the octogenarian. The golfing world had three wonderful examples of competence and confidence paying dividends for three unheralded players in 2003.

Ben Curtis, the 396th ranked player in the world, holed an 8-foot putt on the 18th hole of the Royal St. George's Golf Club at Sandwich, Kent, UK to win the 2003 British Open Championship for his first PGA Tour victory.

Hilary Lunke, who had never finished higher than 15th in twenty-two LPGA events, holed a 15-foot birdie putt on the 18th hole to win a playoff for the 2003 U.S. Women's Open Championship for her first LPGA victory.

Shaun Micheel, winless in 163 previous PGA starts and ranked number 169 in the world, hit a 7-iron approach shot 175 yards from the first cut of the rough to within two inches of the pin on 18th, and then birdied the hole to win the 2003 PGA Championship for his first PGA victory.

Curtis, Lunke, and Micheel all demonstrated competence and confidence in their play in what for each of them had to be a high-stress situation. It was their practiced competence—that is, their muscle memory—and their confidence that carried the day. This same kind of unconscious competence and confidence carries the day for real leaders.

A person once said to me, "Confidence, that's just a bigger word for ego." Wrong! A confident leader doing the right things is not on an ego trip but rather moves forward secure in the understanding that his or her confidence is grounded in a developed competence.

I have often wondered about the competence and confidence of CEOs and other high-level executives who, for example, address their total management team regarding the status of the organization only if their remarks are tightly scripted. Why can't they speak candidly in their own words about what they should know best. Very suspicious! Observing this behavior never raised my confidence level in their competence.

The Professional

A human resource (HR) professional was directly responsible to the CEO for the management of the progression and succession planning of senior company executives. She handled the charting and updating for the CEO, served as an information source, and played devil's advocate in their discussions. This function was obviously "top secret." Only the CEO and the HR professional knew the details of the plan.

The HR professional did not report directly to the CEO in matters other than progression and succession. Her boss did report directly to the CEO and was responsible for several functions, including HR. His competence level in HR lagged well behind his confidence level, or in this case his ego. Further, he was obviously a person who had to be considered in the progression and succession planning process. Yet he thought that he and not his subordinate should be handling the process. He outwardly expressed his displeasure with her involvement and constantly pressured her for information contained in the plan. She steadfastly kept her confidence with the CEO. Her boss, in turn, reflected in his actions a lack of confidence in his ability to compete fairly with his peers as well as a lack of confidence in the CEO and his own HR person to professionally manage a very important and delicate process.

Yes-Man

The decision had been made to get rid of a product that was not performing to expectations. One manager, Roberts, believed a joint venture with another company to develop the market for the product was a better option. So, she convinced the CEO to look at the idea together with Adams, the manager in charge of the product in question. The CEO, however, said, "Adams won't really help us."

The CEO then scripted how the meeting should go. He would initially oppose continuing the product and Adams would agree. Then Roberts was to express the joint venture idea and the CEO would seem to support it. And Adams would agree.

When the meeting was held, Adams reacted exactly as the CEO predicted. The CEO had read him perfectly. Adams was a pure yes-man without confidence in his own competency.

Situations similar to the Professional and the Yes-Man occur all too frequently at all organization levels. They are the result of undeveloped leadership competence and resulting lack of confidence.

Perfect Practice

Unconscious leadership competence may be difficult to attain, but it should be the goal of every leader. Golfers, even Tiger Woods, need and seek help to achieve and maintain the highest level of competence.

Claude "Butch" Harmon is Tiger's coach at this writing. According to Harmon, as quoted in a *Newsweek* magazine article, "the toughest challenge is what's between the golfer's (substitute leader's) ears. It's crucial to have someone skillful teach you right from wrong. Practice makes permanent. It's perfect practice that makes perfect."[3]

Leaders need help in developing their competence, and thus their confidence, whether they are leadership "Tigers" or, like most of us, just struggling to do our best. There is help out there provided we have the humility and courage look for it. And it won't cost hundreds of dollars an hour to get it! Seek out people whose opinions you respect, counsel with people who want you to succeed as a leader, study and learn from people who approach leadership differently from you but who are viewed as effective and respected leaders, and ask other associates in your 360-degree sphere of influence for their perceptions of your leadership effectiveness.

Many golf jokes refer to God's and/or the Devil's intervention. There will be no divine, or devilish, influence to grant you the competitive leadership edge of competence and confidence. It will only come through awareness of what is, and what is not, important to the pursuit of leadership effectiveness, knowledge of how you are perceived as a leader, and perfect practice of the fundamentals. Next we'll tee up performance expectations.

Serenity (confidence) is knowing that your worst shot is still going to be pretty good.

Johnny Miller, 1973 U.S. Open champion, NBC-TV golf analyst

Quick Tips for Improving Your Leadership Game

Real leaders typically understand and model the following in their day-to-day actions:

- Do what's right because it's right.
- If you make a mistake, admit it.
- Trust your associates to take the next step. Send a clear message, "You can do it."
- Make sure your associates know what to do, know how to do it, and have the necessary skills and resources. Then have faith it will be done.

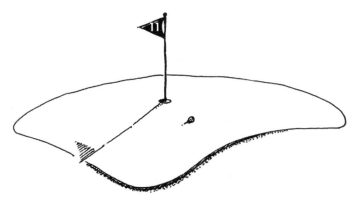

Performance
Expectations

Over the years, (Annika Sorenstam) has developed a
simple philosophy. She will not show up for a
tournament unless she thinks she can win it.[1]

Michael Bamberger, Sports Illustrated

Stevie Wonder and Tiger Woods meet and are discussing their
careers. Woods asks Wonder, "How's the singing career
going?"

Stevie replies, "Not too bad. How's the golf?"

Tiger answers, "Not too bad. I've had some problems with
my swing but I think I've got it taken care of now."

Stevie says, "I always find that when my swing goes wrong,
I need to stop playing for a while and not think about it. Then
the next time I play it seems to be all right."

Tiger exclaims, "You play golf?!"

Stevie replies, "Oh, yes, I've been playing for years."

"But you're blind!" Tiger says. "How can you play golf if you can't see?"

And Stevie replies, "I get my caddie to stand in the middle of the fairway and call to me. I listen for the sound of his voice and play the ball toward him. Then, when I get to where the ball lands, my caddie moves to the green or farther down the fairway and again I play the ball toward his voice."

"But, how do you putt?" asks Tiger.

"Well," says Stevie, "I get my caddie to lean down in front of the hole and call to me with his head on the ground and I just play the ball toward his voice."

Tiger asks, "What's your handicap?"

And to Tiger's amazement, Stevie replies, "Well, I'm proud to say I'm a scratch golfer. (A scratch golfer is one whose handicap is zero. Expect him to shoot par for the course.)

An incredulous Woods, says, "We've got to play a round sometime."

"Well, people don't take me seriously," Wonder replies, "so I only play for money, and never play for less than $10,000 a hole."

Tiger thinks about it and says, "OK, I'm game for that. When would you like to play?"

Stevie says, "Pick a night."

Golfers want to be able to keep score. They want to keep track of how they're doing. They do not want to play in the dark! The rules of golf require accurate scorekeeping. Every golf course has established expectations for each hole on the course. The expectations are clearly specified on the scorecard. The golfer knows how he or she is doing with each stroke.

Performance expectation and actual performance are clear to all. Golfers try to do their best. The results of their efforts are not at all subjective.

Leaders want to be able to keep score as well. So do their followers. In order to keep score in the leadership game, it is imperative that all players be clear about their performance expectations. They need to know, and understand, the expectations. They also need to know how to achieve them, how they will be measured, and the benefits of achieving them. Hopefully, they will agree with the expectations, but in any case they should know the consequences of not meeting them.

Education at Its Best

Years ago I had the pleasure of introducing the noted author and consultant Dr. Ken Blanchard to a group of Owens-Illinois executives and managers. As part of his commentary, Ken told of his early teaching experiences as a university professor. He indicated that his teaching practices were the subject of consternation among the faculty.

Dr. Blanchard proceeded to tell us that on the first day of class he would hand out the final exam and clearly indicate to the class that the exam contained what they needed to learn from his course. If they showed up for class, paid attention, and took notes, they would be able, each and everyone, to get an "A" for the course. And it was his objective that they would all get an "A." Well, as you might expect, Dr. Blanchard's students did very well. This violated the faculty belief in the necessity for a normal distribution of grades!

What was Ken Blanchard doing when he handed out the final exam on the first day of class? He was setting expectations for himself and each member of the class. He was saying, "My job is to teach. Your job is to learn. I expect to do my job and expect you to do yours. At the end of the semester, if you get an "A" we will both be successful.

Fast Start?

You may remember the "values" message sent by managers with the Blessing/White *Fast Start* program mentioned at the 6th hole. The message was that in two-thirds of the eighty to ninety of the cases I have observed, managers were unwilling, unable, uncaring, unbelieving, or just too lazy to prioritize the opportunity to support their new associates getting off to a good start. The principal objective of the *Fast Start* program is that "participants clarify the purpose of their group and individual performance expectations early on." A person new to the game of golf needs some basic help in getting started. So do you as a leader. So do your followers. If you go out and start hitting golf balls when you've never done it before and don't know what you are expected to do, you probably won't do very well. Why wouldn't you think you'd get a similar result if you don't meet your leadership responsibility of establishing performance expectations for your followers? And while we're here, what agreed-upon understandings do you have with your manager regarding your performance expectations? If you have any questions about what is expected of you, take a break from reading and go talk to the boss!

In my experience, a major failing of organizational leaders lies in not providing people a clear understanding of what is expected. And if they do, they often do not offer help in how to meet expectations. Further, they do a poor job of specifying how performance to expectations will be measured. If the expectation is not clear, the measurement cannot be specified. Hence outcomes are unpredictable. I attribute this failing of leadership to the leader's lack of a disciplined approach to establishing performance expectations. The result is one of serendipity best described by the often repeated, and variously attributed, "If you don't know where you are going, any road will get you there." Several examples come to mind.

No How

The plant manager calls a meeting of all supervisors to discuss an across-the-board cost reduction of 10 percent. The plant manager explains that times are tough, sales are down, and central office is putting the pressure on operations to reduce expenses. Deadline for submitting the plant's schedule of reductions is one week from today. The reduction is to include a 10 percent reduction in head count.

The plant manager then asks, in the same not-so-conversational tone in which he has conducted the meeting, ``Are there any questions?'' There are none. People leave the meeting and in the hallway are heard to comment, ``And just how the (expletive deleted) are we supposed to do this?''

Not in These Playing Conditions

Over the previous twenty years, quality had not been a priority. Business was good and the product seemed to be okay. But now the competition was putting pressure on sales, and the market was making a big deal out of product quality. So, company management and the union concluded that quality had to become a priority. A lot of pronouncements from the top, poster campaigns, and a big ad campaign followed, emphasizing the company dedication to producing quality products.

The new emphasis worked well during forty-hour weeks. However, when Saturday and Sunday overtime was required, which was most weeks, the emphasis fell by the wayside. Saturday and Sunday work required the equalization of overtime hours within the total hourly workforce. This was required by the union-management contractual agreements. An employee could have up to thirty hours more overtime than other employees but at that point could not work until the hours were equalized. As a result, assemblers, machine operators, and skilled trades from across the plant were mixed together to continue weekend production. Uppermost in the mind of management was the amount of weekend production that could be accomplished. So, come Monday morning the questions asked related to numbers of units and not product quality. The best production numbers were always on the weekends. Unit numbers were always up at least 10 percent over weekdays. Quality inspectors passed everything. Poor quality couldn't be traced due to the make-shift crews.

Everyone in the plant knew what was going on. The quality posters hung from the walls seven days a week. Leadership did not walk-the-talk.

The Calendar Says Meet

Many organizations conduct regularly scheduled meetings. In the university environment, I was obliged to attend a weekly dean's council meeting. As in the previous example, where employees met weekly to discuss quality issues—and probably not unlike similar activity in your organization—there were established agendas. The meetings had been conducted on a particular day, at a particular time, for years. The meetings were the performance expectation. If you met regularly on Tuesdays, and something happened on a Wednesday, you had to wait until the next Tuesday to get together with the group. "Meet when needed" was not the performance expectation.

Can You Be Trusted?

Leaders often hinder their followers' success by simply not placing trust in them. These leaders would not do well in Las Vegas. When I ask groups of leaders the question, "Can you be trusted?" the response is always an emphatic, "yes."

When I ask, "Can your people be trusted?"

"Well, mostly."

"What do you mean, mostly?"

"Mostly" comes out at 90 percent or higher. If this is true, or even if it is a lesser percentage, say 75 percent or even 60 percent, why do so many leaders expect their followers to earn their trust? Seems to me, with these percentages or "probabilities," the betting leader should follow the advice of the ancient philosopher, Lao Tzu, "Trust first, trust is in the giving."

The best way for the leader to influence trust is to give it and then observe how it is respected by his or her followers. While it is common sense for the leader to give trust, it is also imperative to recognize that the leader must constantly earn the trust of those who follow. Clear and mutually understood performance expectations and agreed upon measurements are key to the issue of trust.

Pre-Shot Routine

All good golfers have a pre-shot routine. Many are so tuned to their routines that if interrupted, they will stop and begin the routine process over again from the beginning. Leaders can benefit from this type of habit. The responsibility for developing performance expectations lends itself to the development of a pre-shot routine. A well-thought-out routine, learned and developed through practice and repetition, and practiced consistently in situations involving the establishment of performance expectations, will greatly enhance the follower's opportunity for success and thereby the leader's. The following is such a routine. It has been recommended in leadership development programs for years.

■ *Step One*: Describe the task in terms of major outcomes and how it fits into the big picture of organizational outputs, goals, and objectives. What, specifically, is to be accomplished.

■ *Step Two*: Agree on measurable criteria for determining that expectations are being met. Emphasize both *agreement* and *measurable*. Identify what specific measurements will indicate success.

■ *Step Three*: Mutually identify the necessary skills, resources, and guidelines required for expected performance. Specify how the performance expectations can be met and what help will be necessary to succeed.

■ *Step Four*: Determine the priorities for action. In order to WIN, you need to do What's Important Now.

■ *Step Five*: Review steps one through four to ensure understanding and commitment. Not a head-nodding to your review; let them do it.

■ *Step Six*: Set a date to review progress. Leave the door open to provide help when necessary.

There is no guarantee of success on the golf course. There is no guarantee of leadership success. However, when the expectations for the game are clearly understood, and the tools of the game are appropriately applied, chance for golfing success is good. Similarly, when the leader establishes clear expectations and ensures that appropriate tools are available, leadership success is more readily achieved.

WIN-win

As leaders we need to be realistic about our own expectations of success. Virtually everything in life is a negotiation. As we discussed at hole #8, Focus, there is little we can control aside from ourselves but much we can potentially influence. Ron Shapiro and Mark Jankowski, authors of *The Power of Nice* and agents for star athletes, offer a technique used in successful deal-making that can aid in achieving our expectations for leadership success. It's what they call "WIN-win." According to Shapiro and Jankowski:

> The best way to get the most of what you want is to help [others get what they want]. It's what we call WIN-win. Both parties win, but you win bigger. It's not WIN-lose. . . . The cliché "win-win" is unrealistic. WIN-win is realistic. One [side] is bound to get more, even if both sides are content with the outcome. . . . Focus on your one most important goal. . . . Help the other side get what it wants as well. . . . Build relationships rather than make one time deals.[2]

Golf makes good use of the WIN-win concept. Every professional tournament has a WINNER. Other participants win as well in earnings, top-10 finishes, tour exemptions, qualification for other tournaments, and so on.

The true measure of a leader's success is the success of his or her followers. The following is my definition of leadership. Obviously I think it's a good one. I'll tell you why.

Leadership is the art of enabling others to achieve success.

There is little disagreement over leadership being an art and not a science. Sure, there are some scientific management tools that help the leader, much as there are in golf. The golfer's clubs, balls, and even attire are designed to maximize golfing efficiency. Frederick W. Taylor's *The Principles of Scientific Management* and W. Edwards Deming's *The Deming System of Profound* Knowledge, among others, have contributed scientific management approaches to the running of organizations. These are certainly helpful to the process. In the end, however, it is the artistry of the golfer, or the leader, and the effective use of the tools of their art, that make the difference.

The "artist" in our "Tuesday Group" is Dick Rice. Dick has an Ernie Els-type swing. It is so smooth, so consistent, and so successful that some of us often loudly and enviously refer to his shot-making as "borrrrrrrrrrrrring."

Enable for Success

We can hand someone a golf club and a golf ball and tell that person to play the game. Similarly, in our leadership role, we can hand a person an assignment and tell him or her to complete the assignment. Managers, not leaders, do this every day. The person with the golf tools may be able to play the game. Similarly, the follower may be able to complete the assignment. Or both may fail! It's the old notion of "sink or swim." Risky business in a global marketplace!

As a golfer, or a leader, failure is not an acceptable objective. Success is! So, instead of just delegating, or dumping, the responsibility to play the game, the golfer and the leader must be enabled. This means both must not only be given the power to act but must be made able, meaning they must be provided with the means (skills, tools, instruction, support, etc.), to succeed at the assignment.

Some golfers learn to play the game through a combination of natural ability and trial and error. More receive instruction from accomplished players or professional instructors. The combination of instruction and practice enables golfers to play the game. Performance on the course measures their skill (success) level.

Do I Make Myself Clear?

Too many individuals placed in leadership positions learn the leadership game through trial and error. Too often they learn an emphasis on doing rather than on leading. The fact that the success of the leader rests on the success of his or her followers is not brought front and center. The responsibility to develop all the good people, not just the best, is too often not a number one priority. Get lazy about doing your people's work, do your leadership work!

You need to include yourself in the responsibility to develop all the good people. Ask your manager, "What performance expectations do you have for me?" Insist on measurable specifics. Don't accept a brush-off. Ask yourself, "What are my expectations?" List them and analyze them. Are they realistic? How will you achieve them? How will you measure your progress in achieving them? After all, if you can't get your own expectations clear in your mind how can you make them clear to your people. And don't assume you know them, check them out periodically with your leader.

Great Expectations

Ben Curtis entered play in the 132nd British Open as an improbable potential winner. Even his caddy had never heard of him. After all, he was a rookie on the PGA Tour and ranked 396th in the world. It was his first major tournament and no one had won a major in their first attempt since Francis Ouimet in 1913. In fact, Curtis hadn't won any PGA Tour tournaments. But win he did with one of the most unforgettable performances in golf history.

He may have been the only person who expected he would win, or might win, or even thought it a possibility he could win!

Great expectations are not always met. In the case of the real leader, the great expectations for leadership success should be there, even though they may not always be realized. You never know, you may pull a "Ben Curtis."

The Leader Is Responsible

The leader is responsible for the success or failure of his or her people. Just as golfers are responsible for their swing and the results of each golf shot, leaders are responsible for the actions taken to enable the success of their followers. If the efforts result in follower success, the leader is successful. If the leader exhausts all possibilities to enable follower success and the follower still fails, then the follower is responsible for the failure and whatever organizational action results from it, such as demotion, transfer, or release. If the leader does not make every reasonable effort to enable follower success, then the leader is responsible if the follower fails and can rightly be blamed for the failure.

The golfer, having swung the club, learns almost immediately whether the shot is successful or not. The leader who enables the success of others cannot expect immediate measurement of success or failure. However, the leader will learn in time that enabling the success of others is the key to personal leadership success and ultimate personal satisfaction.

The golfer who hits the great shot and the leader who experiences a follower's success enjoy the same great sense of satisfaction from having made it happen! "A's all around."

The trouble that most of us find with the modern matched sets of clubs is that they don't really seem to know any more about the game than the old ones did.[3]

Robert Browning

Quick Tips for Improving Your Leadership Game

Real leaders typically understand and model the following in their day-to-day actions:

- You *must* communicate not only the WHAT but the HOW of performance expectations.
- *Remember*: What you measure and reward is what you get!
- Practice the KISS principle, i.e., Keep It Simple, Stupid!
- Help associates who have mastered their present jobs to understand the skill requirements and selection criteria for other jobs in the organization.

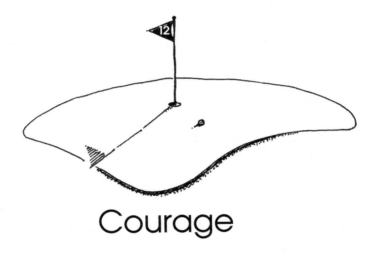

Courage

People don't follow titles, they follow courage.

Sir William Wallace, *Braveheart*

This hunter goes to Africa on a Safari and upon arrival at the hunting lodge he notices there is a golf course. He mentions it to the concierge and indicates if he'd known there was a course he would have brought his golf clubs. The concierge advises that's not a problem, the lodge has every make and model of club, just let him know when he wants to play.

Later, ready to play, our hunter/golfer asks the concierge for a set of Cobra clubs. The next thing he knows, here comes a Zulu caddie with a set of Cobras on one shoulder and a rifle on the other.

The Zulu asks, ``What's your handicap?''

The hunter says, ``12.''

Off they go. On the first hole, he hits his ball into the woods and out comes a hungry lion. The caddie drops the golf bag and shoots the lion with the rifle. The next hole finds our guy in a swampy area and dangling from a tree next to him is a huge asp. Once again, the caddie drops the bag and shoots the asp. The next tee shot finds our guy close to some water and as he prepares his shot an alligator grabs his ankle. Frantically, he hits it with his club and finally he beats it off.

Turning to the Zulu, he asks, ``Why didn't you shoot the alligator?''

And the Zulu caddie replies, ``This is a 13 handicap hole and you don't get a shot.''

Danger Abounds

The game of golf can require courage at times in the face of danger. In fact, the April 1997 issue of *Men's Health* magazine listed the ten most dangerous golf courses around the world. The following are two of their examples:

Lost City Golf Course, Sun City, South Africa. The 13th green is fronted by a stone pit filled with crocodiles, some stretching up to fifteen feet long.

Lundin Links, Fife, Scotland. Enjoyable links near St. Andrews, unless you're Harold Wallace, who in 1950 was hit by a train while crossing the tracks beyond the 5th green.[1]

Golfers face a number of commonplace dangers as they play the game. Sand traps, doglegs, water, trees, rough terrain, out of bounds, heat, cold, rain, and even snow can hamper play. Blind tee shots, where the golfer cannot see the target green, especially when played for the first time, are cause for concern. The danger feared most by golfers, however, is not part of any course. It is lightning. The open areas and trees of golf courses are ideally suited to lightning strikes. Each year a significant number of golfers are struck by lightning, injured, and sometimes killed. What do golfers do to avoid lightning strikes? They suspend play and get off the course. Of course!

The game of leadership also has its hazards, sometimes not as readily observed as are those in golf. The leader is best served to avoid hazards where possible just as the golfer seeks to avoid them, especially the lightning strikes. When the hazard must be faced, the wise leader weighs the risks, proceeds in courageous, albeit cautious, fashion, and is prepared to handle and/or prevent contingencies that may arise.

Who Scheduled This Trip?

The pilot announced the beginning of our landing approach. I looked out the plane window to my right and saw a forest of trees and quickly looked to the left where I saw blue sky. We corkscrewed down to a landing. Welcome to Olaya Herrera Regional Airport, Medellin, Colombia. VFR (visual flight rules) landings only.

After clearing customs, Cliff Shinn, an HR associate, and I took a taxi to the Hotel InterContinental. I noticed the hotel stood in a fenced compound. Not surprising as at the time Medellin was the center of the Colombian Cartel, the so-called drug and murder capital of the world. I was not disappointed to see the fence. Cliff and I were both runners—okay, joggers—and ran in every country we visited while carrying out our international responsibilities for Owens-Illinois Inc. Our run would be accomplished—inside the fence.

The purpose of our trip was a visit to Peldar, O-I's Colombian glass manufacturing affiliate. Our host, Pepe Corujo, general manager of Peldar, came to take us to dinner. He was not driving. His chauffeur, a.k.a. bodyguard, drove. As we rode into Medellin, I noticed something else. Two men in a four-wheel-drive vehicle, early SUV, were closely following us. The passenger held an automatic weapon at the ready.

Following dinner, Pepe took us to his home. It was located in an obviously affluent part of the city. However, as we approached the house, I couldn't see much of it. It was surrounded by a ten- to twelve-foot high stone or concrete wall topped by razor wire. Floodlights lit up the house and lot.

Welcome to life in some parts of the world, where leaders are asked to play the Global Leadership Game. Pepe was definitely playing the leadership game from out of the rough. There will always be extreme difficulties in certain parts of the world that at times will put leaders at additional risk. The ``War on Terror'' increases these risks. It will take courage, the kind of courage Pepe Corujo exhibited each and every day as he met his responsibilities at Peldar, to lead in these environments.

You Gotta Have Heart

Courage is often attributed to professional golfers when they play a difficult shot or select a risky shot rather than take a safer alternative. Their willingness to do so is admired. They are showing "heart," faith in oneself, and confidence—hopefully not desperation!

Who could question the courage, the "heart," and the self-confidence of David Toms as he played a lay-up shot, i.e., an attempt to position the ball for a better, higher percentage shot, on the 18th and final hole of the 2001 PGA Championship Tournament. He then hit the resulting approach shot opportunity close to the pin and one-putted for a one stroke victory over Phil Mickleson! Toms' approach was deliberate and thoughtful. He was cool, calm, and collected.

Sergio Garcia finished second to Tiger Woods at the 1999 PGA Championship Tournament. Golf fans well remember the spectacular shot he made to one of the finishing greens to keep his championship hopes alive. He hit an iron shot from beside a tree with the ball nestled among some tree roots. It was a daring shot, a courageous shot, a prayerful shot as his closed eyes attest as he hit the ball. It worked, and his display of intensity, followed by his unbounded enthusiasm as he raced up the golf course to see the result of his effort, is one of the classic moments of PGA history.

And remember the courage displayed by Annika Sorenstam, the world's best female golfer, in accepting the invitation to play the PGA's 2003 Bank of America Colonial Tournament. In accordance with PGA standards, she played from the men's tees. She narrowly missed the cut and did herself, and the LPGA, proud with her play.

It may be hyperbole to compare electing to take a more difficult golf shot, or play to more difficult standards, with having the courage to step up to leadership decisions affecting the very lives of others. However, just as each golf shot requires a decision to be made, so does each leadership action. One must commit to a shot, a decision, and take action. Once the decision is made you need to have the courage to see it through and make it work. Indecision in golf, as in leadership, almost always leads to a poor shot, a poor action.

The word courage comes from the same stem as the French word "coeur," meaning "heart." It is the foundation that underlies and gives reality to all other virtues and values. Courage is the capacity to move ahead even in the face of despair.

Courage is centered within our being. Without it, our values would wither away. Courage is an assertion of self, a commitment to reality. It is the exercise of integrity. It's doing what is right in the face of personal, political, economic, and/or career risk. A man or woman becomes fully human through his or her choices and commitment to them. People attain worth and dignity from the multitude of decisions they make from day to day. Many of these decisions require courage.

Brave and Courageous

The tragic events of September 11, 2001 changed life in the United States forever. Many people demonstrated leadership on that day. Examples of "just ordinary folks" stepping up and accepting challenges will long be remembered. There were many demonstrations of leadership courage.

Who can forget the final words of Todd Beamer's cell phone call, "let's roll," as he and others moved to successfully stop the terrorists aboard American Airlines Flight 93?

Who can forget Michael and Roselle, who worked on the 78th floor of the World Trade Center? After the planes struck, they descended 78 flights of stairs to safety. As Michael said in a television interview, "we saved each others lives." Their long-time mutual support was never more in evidence. Michael, a blind man, and Roselle, his guide dog, were never closer.

Who can forget the mental image of New York City fire fighters going into the burning World Trade Center and heading "up the stairs." Courage at its ultimate best!

According to Peggy Noonan, writing in the *Wall Street Journal*, "Brave men do brave things. After September 11 a friend of mine said something that startled me with its simple truth. . . . He said, "Everyone died who they were. A guy who ran down quicker than everyone and didn't help anyone—that was him. The guy who ran to get the old lady and was hit by debris—that's who he was. They all died who they were."[2] Their decisions were based on their courage, or lack of it. Their courage was based on their values.

The Willingness to Risk

On #9 we referred to Peter Koestenbaum's *Leadership: The Inner Side of Greatness*. Koestenbaum writes:

> Courage, as a dominant strategy, or dimension, for acquiring the leadership mind, is the willingness to risk. Security . . . lies only in your courage and your character, not in dubious guarantees from the world of business or government or private life. The courageous leadership mind understands that you cannot live life without courage. To lead is to act. To have the courage to take charge, first of one's own life. . . . Then you are ready to take charge of organizations.[3]

Observations of Courage in Action

We have played 11 holes of the Global Leadership Course to this point. We have seen courage in action on virtually every hole we've played. On #3 we saw Meg Mallon report a penalty on herself at the cost of disqualification from an LPGA tournament she was leading.

And, on the same hole, we observed a high school golf coach relinquish a state championship when he noted, and reported, a scoring error.

On hole #4, we tried to imagine the depth of courage required to act by the "whistleblowers" Cooper, Rowley, and Watkins. Also, on #4 we commented on the difficult decisions leaders are required to make to survive in difficult times. Owens-Illinois Inc. cut its worldwide workforce of 80,000 to less than half to manage a takeover and save the company and the jobs of the remaining employees.

Coming down the 5th fairway, we mentioned Neil Armstrong's moon landing adventure, in contrast to the human tragedy of the World War II concentration camps and the courageous spirit of Viktor Frankl. Back on the #6 tee, Bob Dorn stood up and told a group of executives that they, and he, had to change their ways: Survival of the world's largest corporation was at stake.

How many of us would have been able to survive Bill Niehous's ordeal of being held captive in the jungles of Venezuela for three years, as noted when we played #7? We'll read more about Bill's courage when we play #17. On #8, we observed a leader reporting back to his colleagues that the system they as management had put in place, and not paid attention to, was the cause of growing customer complaints. It was not the production workers or front-line supervisors whom they had been blaming, but it was they themselves who were the root cause of the problems. One leader had the courage to stand up, and speak up!

A favorite of mine is the pilot mentioned on hole #9 who simply, and directly, took responsibility before the board of inquiry into his plane's crash by saying, "I screwed up." Also, on #9 we reflected on the corporate courage of Johnson & Johnson's response to the Tylenol scare on the macro scale and a young Navy lieutenant's acceptance of responsibility on the micro scale. When playing the 10th hole, we observed a human resource person maintain her professional confidence with the CEO in the face of pressure from her boss. Finally, on #11, I still wonder whether Tiger would have the courage to play Stevie at night!

There will be more examples of leadership courage as we finish our round. Look for Buck Lipton and Stan Hensley on #13, Bruce Edwards on #16, more on Bill Niehous and also Ernest Shackleton on #17.

Stay Calm, Cool, and Collected

Golfers face the potential for despair in attempting to avoid or overcome the dangers of the golfing environment. Often they lose strokes and raise their scores but rarely stomp off the golf course in disgust. Rather they shake off past misfortune and play on. Sammy Rachels, first-time winner on the Senior PGA Tour at the 2001 Bell South Senior Classic on June 3, 2001, is quoted as saying, "Golf is 80 percent mental and 20 percent psychological." Just as the successful golfer maintains control, so too the leader must exercise control and remain calm, cool, and collected. This is the required state for assessing risks and handling crises most effectively.

An Opportunity to Be Courageous

Golfers, professional and amateur alike, are upset when they perform poorly on the golf course. Professionals, more times than not it seems, will finish a round in which they feel they could have played better and immediately head for the driving range or the putting green. Their objective is to iron out the flaw they have detected in their game. Amateurs may not practice immediately after playing but they will replay their round in their mind. They will review missed shots, poor club selection, and any other mistakes they think they made and what they might do differently next time out so that they can play and score better. Some, myself included, will make notes on how to improve and put them in their golf bag for reference before the next tee time. Professional and amateur golfers will not tolerate their own poor golfing performance if there is anything at all they can do to improve it. In contrast, it too often seems that leaders fail to work on a remedy for their own poor performance. They do not reflect on the outcomes of projects, meetings, or events in the same thoughtful, analytic, improvement-seeking manner of the dedicated golfer. Thus remedies for poor performance or understandings of what works are lost.

An example of poor leadership performance that concerns me is the way in which leaders too often deal, or more accurately fail to deal, with a poor performer in their area of organizational responsibility. One specific area of concern is the poor performer with established years of service. People attending leadership sessions complain that these people don't carry their share of the load. Further, they claim they can't do anything about them.

Remember on the previous hole, #11, we said if the leader exhausts all possibilities to enable follower success and the follower still fails, then the follower is responsible for the failure. At this point, the leader needs to exhibit courage, meet his or her responsibilities to the organization and to the nonperformer's colleagues, and take appropriate action. Managers—note I didn't say leaders—argue that they can't get this job done. Apparently they prefer to suffer the poor performer, lay more work on his or her colleagues, blame human resource policies or the union agreement, and set the example for others that poor performance is okay, rather than take some very basic steps to resolve performance issues.

Whether people have simply fallen off the performance wagon, been transferred to you under the disguise of stellar performance ratings, or determined that they have enough years of service to make themselves fire-proof and can coast into retirement, you've got to have the courage to put a stop to their behavior. As William F. Buckley once said on the Larry King television show, "If it is unacceptable behavior, how can you accept it?" Further, to do so will put your organization on the road to mediocrity.

What to Do?

Early in the round, we said leadership, like golf, is a simple game, and that its essence, like that of golf, is skilled execution of key fundamentals. On #6, we said leaders should always focus on the situation, issue, problem, decision, or behavior, and not on the person. Later, as we played #8, we said leaders must deal with the facts and not with their feelings. The facts of poor performance to expectations require implementation of a "performance improvement plan" for the poor performer.

As a leader, you need to go back to the beginning. You need to level with your employee. Performance expectations must be re-affirmed and their clarity ensured. Realistic timetables for a return to improvement should be laid out including a schedule for progress reviews. The employee must understand that the process has only two possible outcomes: one, a return to acceptable performance, or two, removal from the assigned responsibilities, including the possibility of termination of employment. This process should be witnessed and all parties should literally sign off on the plan. Both the employee and the leader must work to make the plan succeed if at all possible. Look at it this way, as the leader you are trying to protect an organizational human resource investment and avoid the high costs of bringing on a replacement.

In my experience, when the above action steps are taken, the chances for the employee's return to an acceptable level of performance are very good. It's the "no one ever explained my situation to me in this way before" reaction. And if poor performance continues, the leader is justified in taking the appropriate action to remove the employee from the assigned responsibilities. The organization, the leader's team, and the poor performer will have been treated fairly and responsibly. And courageously!

Every Day Courage

Courage in the golfing sense is demonstrated by the golfer at various times during any 18-hole round. Opportunities for leaders to demonstrate courage in the organization environment occur virtually every day. They involve the opportunity to do the right thing, make the right decision. They don't make the headlines but have great impact on organization success and failure. Here are a few additional examples of every day leadership courage.

Just Say No

The department head told the accountant, "I want to install an upgrade to our network to include wireless connectivity throughout the facility."

The accountant replied, "You can't buy it now. There's no money in the capital expenditure account to do it. We have no discretionary funds available for that purpose. We would have to take money from other dedicated operational accounts."

"I don't care, I need it. Other facilities have it and I want it. Take the money out of operating expense or find it somewhere else," said the irate manager.

"Look, I've checked purchase alternatives and talked with the comptroller. We shouldn't do it. If you are directing me to do it anyway then put it in writing!" said the accountant.

The department head called the comptroller and got the same response from her that he'd gotten from the accountant. He dropped the request for purchase,

Subsequently, the accountant, on his own initiative worked up a lease-to-own arrangement for the switching equipment. It cost a little more over time but fit into the budgetary constraints. The department head was pleased.

The accountant had the courage to say no and exercised the responsibility to seek an alternative solution.

A Challenge

I remember a discussion with a group of leaders on the subject of "challenging the boss." One of the leaders argued that we need to redefine the relationship between boss and subordinate. What he said was, "People should challenge their bosses with the question, 'why do you require me to do these wasteful things?'" It is an interesting question. Perhaps we could turn it around a bit. Why not ask your team to express their view of wasteful things you and they are required to do? Share those views and your own with your boss. Encourage your team to continually speak up about wasteful activity. They may be right. If not, it points up the need for clarification of why questioned activity is important.

Not a Popularity Contest

The only woman member of the golf club's board had been approached by a majority of the women golfers to arrange for the moving of the tee forward and to the top of a hill on a long par 5 hole. Subsequently, the concerned women sent a letter to the club president requesting the change. During a board meeting, after a great deal of discussion and argument, the president asked for the woman board member's opinion. She said, "The tee should be located where it best serves the interest of all members of the club regardless of gender. Leave it where it is." The tee did stay where it was. The woman board member's input to the board was not popular with many of the women golfers. She knew it wouldn't be when she expressed her view but thought it was the right thing to do.

Now let's look at courage's close cousin, "guts."

Now This Took Guts!

My nephew, Michael McHugh, recently retired after thirty years of service in the U.S. Navy. All of his assignments had been as part of the submarine force. Captain Mike graduated from the Naval Academy. As a final step to being accepted into the navy's nuclear submarine program, he was interviewed by Admiral Hyman Rickover, the "father" of our nuclear navy. This interview was required of all officer candidates who had passed all other selection hurdles. Admiral Rickover, by reputation, was an irascible, no-nonsense, blunt, pragmatic workaholic, "who took no prisoners."

Mike passed his interview with the admiral. After all, he had an engineering degree from the Academy. He's personable, disciplined, and deferential, and one could easily see why he had no difficulty meeting and being accepted by the admiral.

However, another applicant faced a much more difficult interview with Admiral Rickover. As Mike relates, another young ensign reached the final interviewstage, the meeting with the admiral. This officer was not a Naval Academy graduate.

As the young man entered the admiral's Pentagon office and came to attention in front of Rickover's desk, he noted the amount of work stacked in piles all across the massive desk. While the ensign stood at attention, Admiral Rickover leafed through his personnel file and then, abruptly looked up and said, ``What are you doing here?''

Before the young officer could answer, Rickover said, ``You're not an engineer, you've got a degree in psychology! Why would I even think of accepting you into the nuclear program? All that psychology bunk and I'll bet you couldn't even make me mad!''

The ensign, obviously surprised by the admiral's behavior, nonetheless maintained his military posture as he gazed at Rickover. Several long seconds passed. Then the ensign broke his stance of attention, walked over to the end of the admiral's desk, extended his right arm and in one great sweeping motion cleared everything off the desk: papers, folders, pictures, letter openers, pen set, nameplate, etc.!

Before the last paper had settled to the floor, Admiral Rickover, in what Mike describes as one indiscernible move, vaulted from his chair to a standing position on his desk. He was totally outraged! And he ordered the ensign out of his office.

Subsequently, Admiral Rickover, approved the ensign's request for assignment to the submarine force and training as a nuclear submarine officer.

The ensign's decision and action took a lot of courage in addressing the admiral's challenge. Admiral Rickover confirmed his own integrity by honoring that expression of courage and accepting the young officer.

Obviously, the ensign and the admiral illustration is not commonplace. Unfortunately, in my experience neither is the expression of individual leadership courage. Simply put, leadership courage is about doing what is appropriate and right and having the "guts" to act.

Another Short Self-Assessment

Back on hole #4, Play by the Rules, you had the opportunity to assess yourself on leadership ethics. I suggest you score yourself again, this time on some of the leadership skills associated with "courage." Use Figure 12-1 as your scorecard. As with the "ethics" self-assessment, follow a forced distribution to score yourself, i.e., rank order the skills from 5 (most effective) to 1 (least effective). Your scoring will provide a measure of relative effectiveness on these skills.

Once again, if you have scored yourself, it was probably difficult to work out the forced distribution. Hopefully, the process generated some insight into your quest to be a courageous leader. As with the ethics assessment, you may wish to ask others to rate you, using the same forced distribution. Any difference between their perception of your leadership courage and your own evaluation is important for you to know and analyze.

Center of Moment

The "center of moment" is a nautical term. It refers to that precise moment at which a vessel reaches the point in a rolling motion when it will either right itself or capsize. Life for the leader is full of these "centers of moment." Courage is required to address them.

Courage causes the real leader to do the right thing when confronted by being in the right place at the wrong time or the wrong place at the right time. The real leader is not afraid to be exposed, overcomes the uneasy feeling when walking among the enemy, and does not fail to lead because there is too much "work" or too many other "organization things" to do.

FIGURE 12-1.
Sample leadership courage assessment.

As a leader, I:

_____ Make hard choices and address difficult situations.

_____ Stand alone when needed.

_____ Take necessary corrective actions.

_____ Remain cool under fire.

_____ Take risks willingly.

Using a forced distribution, rank order the skills from 1 (least effective) to 5 (most effective), according to the following leadership effectiveness scale:

1—Least effective

2—Less effective

3—Acceptable

4—More effective

5—Most effective

SOURCE: Adaptive Leader Consulting Associates, Ltd., *Adaptive Leader Skills Assessment.* Copyright 1994.

What Political Game Do You Play?

In the organizational environment, the situations you confront may seem inconsequential and not related to courage. First, allow me to say, all the actions of a leader are consequential. Now, let me ask, do you have the courage to avoid behavior such as the following:

- Maneuvering situations and people for personal advantage or gain?
- Currying the approval of those in power?
- Shading the facts to your benefit?
- Being the proverbial yes-woman or yes-man?

■ Invoking the boss's name to influence action rather than exercising your own authority?

The above behaviors are not mortal sins. They are just habitual ways of adapting to perceived demands of the organization or to your own perception of how to get ahead. The price paid for such behavior is both organizational and personal. Each such act shaves a thin slice off our integrity. The cumulative effect is loss of trust and organizational mediocrity. Have the courage to play the politics of the greater good, not the politics of personal power! As Pope John Paul II often said, "Be not afraid."

Brave people need to be nurtured and valued in organizations. We need brave leaders, now and in the future. Courage provides competitive edge. It helps you apply your professional skills as you should, to maintain your integrity, and to be an authentic real leader. All other things being equal, as a person and a leader in the global market place playing the global leadership course, courage is the edge!

Courage is rightly esteemed the first of human qualities
. . . because it is the quality that guarantees all others.

Winston Churchill

Quick Tips for Improving Your Leadership Game

Real leaders typically understand and model the following in their day-to-day actions:

■ Take calculated risks. Ask yourself, "What is the worst thing that can happen?" and then decide whether proceeding is worth the risk.

■ Create a climate in your group/organization in which conflict is freely expressed. Conflict not expressed means problems are not being confronted.

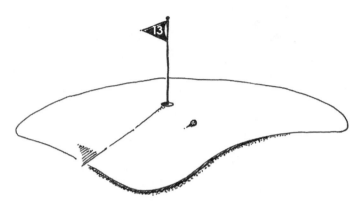

Recognize Positive Results

The competitor entitled to play first from the teeing ground is said to have the "honor."

Official Rules of Golf, Rule 10, Order of Play

A dignified English solicitor and widower with a considerable income had long dreamed of playing Sandringham, one of Great Britain's most exclusive golf courses. One day, while traveling in the area, he made up his mind to chance it and see if he could play the course.

Upon entering the clubhouse, he asked at the desk if he might play the course. The club secretary inquired, ''Member?''

''No, sir.''

''Guest of a member?''

''No, sir.''

''Sorry.''

Disappointed, the lawyer turned to leave. As he did so he spotted a slightly familiar figure seated in the lounge, reading the *London Times*. It was Lord Parham. He approached and, bowing low, said, ``I beg your pardon, your Lordship, but my name is Higginbotham of the London solicitors Higginbotham, Willingby, and Barclay. I should like to crave your Lordship's indulgence. Might I play this beautiful course as your guest?''

His Lordship gave Higginbotham a long look, put down his paper and asked, ``Church?''

``Church of England, sir, as was my late wife.''

``Education?''

``Eton, sir, and Oxford.''

``Sport?''

``Rugby, sir, a spot of tennis and Number Four on the crew that beat Cambridge.''

``Service?''

``Brigadier, sir, Coldstream Guards, Victoria Cross and Knight of the Garter.''

``Campaigns?''

``Dunkirk, El Alamein, and Normandy, sir.''

``Languages?''

``Private tutor in French, fluent German, and a bit of Greek.''

His Lordship considered briefly, then nodded to the club secretary, and said, ``Nine holes.''

Humility

Most people are not impressed by the recitation of the credentials of others. We prefer people to be humble. Humility is a magic word. Golf is a most humbling diversion. No person—whether a champion, a top professional, or a leading money winner—ever reaches the point of saying, "I have learned the secret. I have conquered this bewitching, bedeviling game!" When confidence is at its peak and satisfaction with one's game brings great joy, golf will let you have it. You'll slice, or hook, your drive into the rough, or the woods, or even out of bounds. You'll struggle to get back to the fairway. Your approach shot will come up short. You will "air-mail the green" (fly your ball over it), or land in a sand trap in the "fried egg position" (the ball is plugged into the sand and it really does look like a fried egg). Then you four-putt for a score considerably over par. You will be chastened. You will know humility!

Once again, leadership parallels golf. It, too, is full of humbling experiences. Achievement and recognition are here today and gone tomorrow. You know, the familiar message, "What have you done for me lately?" Thus, it is best to approach the game of leadership in the humble manner also suited to the game of golf, i.e., modestly, unpretentiously, calmly, and always consciously aware of our shortcomings. The key element in humility is honesty. It assumes no undue reward or attention. It is the avoidance of pomposity and addiction to the limelight.

Many leaders shy away from recognition. I almost believe it is a characteristic of "real leadership." They know they are leaders and that is enough. We need to be aware of this shyness and approach recognition for such folks in an appropriate way.

Meeting a "Real Hero"

I met Carwood "Buck" Lipton at a meeting of Owens-Illinois Inc. international managers in Geneva, Switzerland. He was a handsome man of average height, quick to smile, and with a shock of snow-white hair. My immediate impression was this is a very nice man. It was years later that I learned he was a hero of no small proportion when he and his *Band of Brothers* were immortalized by author Steven Ambrose.

Buck Lipton was a combat paratrooper in World War II. He served in Easy Company, 506th Regiment, 101st Airborne. Easy Company had 147 members and was engaged in the war from the Normandy landing to the capture of Hitler's "Eagle's Nest" fortress. Buck trained as a private, fought in combat as a corporal and sergeant, and received a battlefield commission to 2nd lieutenant. He was one of only four noncommissioned officers who were present and accounted for every day of Easy Company's three-year wartime existence. Buck Lipton was awarded the Bronze Star for his actions on D-Day.

Buck Lipton, and many others like him, performed courageously in World War II as front-line soldiers. It is they who fought to secure eventual victory. It is they who were placed at the point of greatest risk, at "FEBA," the forward edge of the battle area. Their leaders were, for the most part, highly effective as well. All deserve recognition for their extraordinary contributions. Few ask for it. News commentator and author Tom Brokaw called the peers of Buck Lipton "The Greatest Generation" in his best-selling book of the same name.

Recognition: Who Needs It?

The good people, the contributors of every generation, are humble people. They don't seek recognition for their actions. They simply conduct themselves in responsible ways because they are just that, responsible people. Many work on the frontline of the battle for success in a global economy. Though they may not ask for it, they do need recognition for their efforts. We as leaders must provide recognition to the deserving. Our success depends on their efforts. Recognition of their contributions is a major avenue for leadership support. Recognizing the positive results of our followers can help to sharpen the slight edge of individual performance effectiveness.

If you perform as a real leader, I have no doubt you will be recognized for your leadership effectiveness. However, it may be that no one will tell you how effective you are. People are just not inclined to tell the boss, "You are a good leader." But, you will know what you have accomplished. Sometimes it may feel as if you've just scored a hole-in-one without a witness. Who cares, you know you've done it! Humbly accept whatever leadership accolades come your way but never lose your focus on those who really make success happen. Real leaders cause others to succeed because they know that's the secret to achieving maximum success for everyone, including themselves.

Who knows, one day when you are walking through a shopping mall or driving your golf cart on your favorite course you'll hear someone shouting your name. It's one of your former employees and they just want to say hello and ask how are you doing. That tells you something about what kind of leader you were. Smile and enjoy it. It's probably the highest form of recognition you'll ever receive!

Remember Charlie?

You met Charlie Butcher at hole #1. Remember how Charlie, who ran his family's Massachusetts-based cleaning products business, demonstrated over many years his concern for the well-being of the men and women on the shop floor. "He loved to see cars in the parking lot because he knew people were at work."

Bob Kievra, writing in the Worcester, Massachusetts *Telegram & Gazette*,[1] reported on Charlie's reluctant sale on September 18, 2000 of his company to the S.C. Johnson Company of Racine, Wisconsin (coincidentally my hometown). "S.C. Johnson didn't offer the highest bid, but it was the best one for the employees," said Mr. Butcher. According to Paul McLaughlin, president of the Butcher Company, Charlie "had not planned to sell, but when he did, he made it clear that his workers had made the company what it was and they should be rewarded."

"Charlie wanted to take care of his workers," said Had Beatty, who was the company's vice chairman for several years. "Some of them are second generation Butcher workers and he wanted everyone to feel valued."

Charlie came East from his home in Boulder, Colorado to complete the sale on a Monday. Less than twenty-four hours later, he was hand-delivering bonus checks to about 110 Butcher employees at the corporate headquarters in Marlboro. Checks were handed out the same day to workers at the company's production plants in Compton, California and Alsip, Illinois. Bonuses were based upon seniority and position, and were distributed against a backdrop of "tears, hugs, and joyful exclamations." The $18 million paid out to 325 employees averaged more than $55,000 per employee.

Charlie Butcher was described as an unassuming man who shunned the spotlight. Sounds like a humble man to me. According to Paul McLaughlin, "Charlie has a gentle spirit and really loves people. It's nice to know that nice guys don't necessarily finish last."

It was a testament to the leadership of Charlie Butcher and the other leaders of the Butcher Company that, while a few employees took an extended lunch hour on Tuesday, the day the bonuses were delivered, absenteeism was close to 0 percent on Wednesday!

Not Bonuses—Bananas

The sales manager for a medium-size chemical company rushed into the president's office, exclaiming, "We got the Spartan contract we've been working on for four months."

The president was very pleased with the news. Then for no reason apparent to the sales manager, he began looking around the room and going through his desk drawers. Out of the top drawer of the desk, he pulled a banana left over from lunch. "Here," he said, "take this. I know it sounds stupid, but I've got to recognize this great work with something, and right now! This banana is the best I can do. Congratulations!

The sales manager eventually received a more valuable reward for his performance, but perhaps not a more significant one. The company used the incident to establish a "Golden Banana Award." Small gold pins in the shape of a banana became a symbolic reward to be given to employees in recognition of outstanding contributions to the company success. The award became a prized possession of all who earned it.

Stan the Man

The real work of leading people in an organization is not done by the top executives. It is done levels below by people who really have to roll their sleeves up. Trite, but true, and I once knew a real leader who knew this well.

I spent a number of years as a then General Motors Institute representative assigned to the Buick Motor Division in Flint, Michigan. At the time Buick employed over 25,000 people. The majority of them were located at the Buick complex, which ran the length of Flint's Leith Street. A series of plants performed all the operations involved in the manufacture of the various Buick models.

While at Buick, I became familiar with all its operations, including Final Assembly. A gentleman by the name of Stan Hensley was the superintendent of Final Assembly. Stan did not fit the picture many have of a leader. But neither did Sir Winston Churchill, nor in reality do many leaders. Rather they come in all sizes and shapes. Their leadership greatness comes from within. Stan's appearance, as I recall it, is best described as a mixture of Churchill and Alfred Hitchcock. But no one noticed!

Stan believed that his job was to enable his work force, i.e., to make sure they had all they needed to be successful. So, he spent his days, aside from mandatory meetings, walking the plant floor. He greeted people at their work stations, asked how they were doing, and meant it. He talked about their jobs and asked if they needed any help. He listened to their ideas and their complaints. And he got to know them personally in some detail. He had the facility to remember what they told him. He saw that their questions or suggestions were responded to either personally or with help from his staff.

Stan saw to it that everyone in Final Assembly received a birthday card from him. As I recall, there were some 2,000 employees in Final Assembly. He received wedding invitations, baptismal and graduation announcements, and invites to events employees viewed as special. He always responded, sent gifts, or attended ceremonies in recognition of these occasions. Stan attended funerals and wakes, not only of employees but of their spouses and children.

What do you suppose was the response of the people in Buick Final Assembly to Stan Hensley? Simple. They loved him! They did good work! They helped resolve assembly problems! The operation of Final Assembly was a success!

Stan Hensley recognized who did the work, who caused Buick Final Assembly operations to succeed or fail. He spent as much time as he could letting people know how valuable they were and how much he appreciated them. It was his number one priority. How many of you can say the same?

You Can't Be Too Busy

Today's leaders too often overlook the power of recognizing individual and group contributions. They claim to be "too busy," or they simply won't take the time to acknowledge the efforts of others. Everyone craves recognition. It raises feelings of being valued, reassures people that they do make a difference, and inspires good effort. Golfers rarely miss acknowledging a good shot. Why does it appear to be so easy for the golfer to applaud good play and so hard for managers to applaud good work? Leaders also need to recognize good performance as well as good effort, express understanding and concern when things don't go well, and provide for appropriate help when needed.

Golfers try to repeat behaviors that lead to the right results on the golf course. Their successful efforts are recognized by their caddie and/or playing partners, and by the crowd in the case of professionals. Your people deserve no less recognition when their successful performance merits it.

Many organizations have what I call "programmed recognition." They hold pizza parties, offer cash awards, certificates for merchandise, meals, discounts, etc. These can all have their place when used appropriately and sincerely. However, remember leadership is an individual game. You must offer your people recognition from you. And the simplest means—the verbal or written thank you, and the modeling of the "Stan Hensley" approach to recognition—will cost the least and have the biggest payoff.

Another Challenge

Why is giving recognition for positive results difficult for many leaders? Maybe we don't get enough practice! Let's go to the "recognition range" and hit a few. The challenge is for you to identify an opportunity to give an employee some recognition for positive results. Notice the emphasis is on performance expectations, which is where it should be.

1. What is your group accountable for contributing to the organization?
2. Given the contribution your group is expected to make, what behaviors and results are important?
3. Who should be recognized for specific actions and results contributing to meeting group expectations?
4. How will you express your personal appreciation to the person, or team, selected?

And don't stop there, you've probably just begun your "recognition round." Here's something you might try when the circumstances are right. Someone deserves recognition for a specific accomplishment or perhaps really good work over an extended period of time. Take a plain piece of stationery and prepare a short handwritten note of recognition. Sign it and mail it to the employee's home. Who gets the mail at home? Probably a spouse or the kids. Mom or dad comes home and everybody wants to know, "who's the letter from?" And when the contents are read where does the letter go? You've got it, on the refrigerator! You've delivered recognition in front of the audience that really counts, the employee's family.

One thing to remember, golfers do not congratulate their playing partners on poor or bad shots. So, too, the leader should not tell people "good job" when in fact they are not doing a good job! Simply allowing people to do poor or shoddy work is a form of recognition and should be acted upon. To not act indicates approval to perform poorly. Remember what you measure and reward, actively or passively, is what you get.

Work in Progress

My golf shots can land in the fairway, the rough, the woods, the water, or even a sand trap, and in every case I need to consider what club to use for my next shot. What kind of a lie do I have? What is the relationship of my ball to the green? These questions answered, I make my club selection. I will go through this process for the entire round of golf. Leaders need to follow this example when they assign tasks to individuals or teams.

When you assign a task you have high expectations for its completion. Often individuals and/or teams will exceed these expectations. Often they do not. In either case, you should *check in* on the progress being made toward meeting expectations. Those who are exceeding expectations will be reinforced by your recognition of their positive progress. Those who are having difficulty will need your help. They are probably working hard enough and care enough. Their difficulty usually stems from a lack of understanding, or misunderstanding, of the expectations, not having the right tools, or lack of required support. They need you to recognize them with a "how's it going?" You can then respond to their needs. Successful projects need positive reinforcement along the way.

Real leaders know how much "checking in" is appropriate and welcome. They do not want to micromanage and risk people losing task ownership, or stifling innovation and creativity. They will know their people and be able to gauge how much help is needed or not needed. The support will be handled in the same way as a three-foot putt for par. Very carefully!

Classic Recognition

In the early days of professional golf in the United States, golfers were allowed to play country club courses in tournaments but were not granted club house privileges. One of the first, if not the very first, to grant such privileges was the Inverness Country Club in Toledo, Ohio. As the *Toledo Blade* on August 18, 1920 reported:

> Inverness held "open house" for the pros while here, and "open house" meant that the players, professional and amateur, were guests of the club, with all the privileges and every courtesy that is extended to guests. There was absolutely no

line drawn between the amateur and the professional player, as has been done in the past, especially in the east, and the professionals appreciated this democracy, or Toledo spirit, call it what you like.

The occasion was the playing of the 1920 U.S. Open Championship. In recognition of the hospitality shown them by the members of Inverness, the golfers presented the club a magnificent cathedral clock, which has since remained in the foyer of the Inverness Club. The clock bears the following inscription.

This cathedral clock was presented to the Inverness Club by the professional golfers present at the Open Championship of 1920 as a testimonial of their deep appreciation of the many courtesies extended to them and the spirit of genuine democracy which prompted such hospitality.

God measures men by what they are
Not what they in wealth possess
This vibrant message chimes afar
The voice of Inverness

Quick Tips for Improving Your Leadership Game

Real leaders typically understand and model the following in their day-to-day actions:

- Reward excellence and acknowledge and reinforce effort, progress, and growth.
- Give credit when credit is due and be specific about the accomplishment and why it is praiseworthy.
- Acknowledge courageous associates who demonstrate high ethical standards through their behavior.

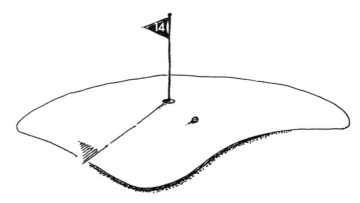

Provide Constructive Feedback

The pat on the back, the arm around the shoulder, the praise for what was done right and the sympathetic nod for what wasn't, are as much a part of golf as life itself.

Former President Gerald R. Ford

On a recent Sunday morning, a husband reluctantly agreed to play in the Couples Alternate Shot Tourney at his golf club. He and his wife were partners, and each would take every other shot as a team.

The husband teed off on the first hole and blistered a drive 300 yards down the middle. Upon reaching the ball, he said to his wife, ``Just hit it towards the green, anywhere around there will be fine.''

The wife proceeded to shank the ball deep into the woods.

Undaunted, the husband said, ``That's okay, sweetheart,'' and spent the full five minutes allowed looking for the ball, finding it just in time in an absolutely horrible position. He played the shot of a lifetime to get the ball within two feet of the hole and told his wife to knock the putt in. The wife proceeded to knock the ball off the green and into a bunker.

Still maintaining his composure, the husband summoned on all his skill and holed the shot from the bunker. He took the ball out of the hole and while walking off the green put his arm around his wife and calmly said, ``Honey, that was a bogey. That's okay but I think we can do better on the next hole.''

To which his wife replied, ``Listen, mister, don't bitch at me. Only two of those five shots were mine.''

Let's play this hole on an "alternate shot" basis as did our husband and wife, except that "you the leader" will be playing with "you the follower." As leader, you are responsible for providing constructive feedback within your 360-degree sphere of influence, with the goal of helping to improve followers, peers, and your leadership, that is, to develop their slight edge. As a follower, you are responsible for developing your own slight edge. You want both of "you" to shoot your best on this hole. It is a tough one and many do not play it as well as they might. As we play along remember the lessons apply to both of "you."

Feedback is defined by *Webster's New World Dictionary and Thesaurus* as "the transfer of part of the output back to the input, as of . . . information." You need to be concerned with feedback, specifically constructive feedback. Constructive feedback is feedback leading to improvement.

One of the unique aspects of the game of golf is that of timely definitive feedback. Dr. Bernard Rosenbaum, author of *How to Motivate Today's Worker*, describes it in the following way:

> Golf provides a textbook case for the efficacy of feedback. There is instant feedback after each shot that serves both motivational and instructional purposes. The feedback is immediate, direct, and goal-related. . . . In a number of golf groups there is a tendency to concede putts if they are within a putter's reach of the cup in order to speed up the game. I have resisted this for I have never failed to appreciate the wonderful sound of the ball falling into the cup as the ultimate feedback of goal attainment on every hole.[1]

The effectiveness of each and every golf shot is undeniable. The measurement of strokes per hole, strokes per round, and over time the measure of a handicap all clearly define an individual golfer's skill level. The golfer may verbally stretch the truth about the quality of his or her game but physically cannot do that when actually playing the game. Performance on the course is readily observed, and that's where its effectiveness is measured. The Professional Golf Association (PGA) maintains statistics for all playing PGA professionals, women and men. Last time I looked there were over fifty measurements of individual play.

As in golf, leadership effectiveness is not determined by what the leader thinks or feels it is. Rather, it is play on the (leadership) course that determines how well the leader is applying his or her skills to the leadership game. The leader's play is observed by followers, peers, bosses, and a host of known and unknown observers.

No Feedback on This One

Feedback is genuinely welcomed by some people. Others don't like to receive any feedback they see as critical; they like only positive comment about their performance. Sometimes we have to give and/or receive feedback that is hard to accept. If it affects performance, the leader is obliged to deliver it. At other times (some would say this happens all too often) we don't get the accolades our performance deserves.

The Reverend Francis woke up one Sunday morning and, realizing it was an exceptionally beautiful and sunny early Spring day, decided he just had to play golf. So he told the associate pastor that he was not feeling very well and asked him to say Mass for him.

As soon as the associate pastor left, Father Francis headed to a golf course about forty miles away. He didn't want to accidentally see any of his parishioners. He was all alone as he prepared to hit his ball on the first tee. After all, it was Sunday morning and everyone else was in church!

At about this time, St. Peter leaned over to the Lord as they observed Father Francis from the heavens and said, ''You're not going to let him get away with this, are you?''

The Lord sighed, and said, ''No, I guess not.'' Just then, Father Francis hit the ball. It flew straight and true toward the green, dropped on the putting surface, rolled toward the pin, and fell into the cup. It was a 420-yard hole-in-one! St. Peter was astonished. He looked at the Lord and asked, ''Why did you let him do that?''

The Lord smiled and replied, ''Who's he going to tell?''

In addition to observations of performance, there are perceptions of performance. Unfortunately the performance of leader and follower alike is too often based on vague impressions, opinions, or organizational politics rather than observed behaviors or substantiated facts. Thus perception plays a major part in the measurement of performance. Perceptions may or may not be accurate, or tell only part of the story. It is best to guard against taking action based solely on perception, especially the perception of others.

The Firing of Ernie B.

Some years ago, I was promoted to the position of an area manager for General Motors Institute. My new residence location was Dayton, Ohio. As I readied for the move, I was advised by the regional manager, my new boss, and by the person I was to replace, that the first thing I needed to attend to was the firing of Ernie B., our in-plant representative at one of the Dayton-area GM divisions.

Ernie had developed a program based on the concept of ``value analysis,'' which was being implemented with great success in his assigned division. The process was literally resulting in sensational dollar savings.

My new boss and my predecessor had asked Ernie on several occasions to document the program for use in other GM divisions. This was certainly a reasonable request. Yet, no documentation was forthcoming. The fussing and fuming over Ernie's failure to provide the program write-up had reached the point of my being directed to fire Ernie. You're right, they were bailing out and giving me their difficult situation. Ever happen to you? Have you done it to someone else? Don't! So, what did I do? I knew Ernie, but only casually. He was by nature outspoken and some would say a bit stubborn, if not bull-headed. My first stop in Dayton was a visit with Ernie in his plant location conference room. It was my intention to conduct a constructive feedback session aimed at a positive result, not a firing.

``Ernie, we have a situation which requires immediate attention. I've been asked to fire you for insubordination for refusing to document the ''value analysis`` activity. Now I know you're doing good work here and the division is very happy with your contribution. I'd like to see you continue that success but you also have a responsibility to our department that's not being met. Unless that responsibility is met your employment is in jeopardy. The higher-ups are upset with your behavior as they should be. What can we do about this?''

Ernie replied. ``I'm too d——d busy doing the program to be writing up reports. 'You know who' is too lazy to come on down here and see what's actually going on. I'm working twelve- to fourteen-hour days and all they can do is get on the phone and jump on me about 'where's the program write-up.' ''

Allow me to shortcut the rest of the conversation, which really didn't take very long. I suggested to Ernie that we work together to complete the program write-up. This would complete the task, make the activity available to others, satisfy the higher-ups, and I would learn what he was doing and could help handle future requests for information. He agreed and we did it.

A few years later, I left General Motors. Ernie continued his career with General Motors Institute until his retirement in the 1990s. He was considered by his colleagues and clients to be a most professional and highly respected facilitator of management development programs. I know I helped make that future success possible by conducting a feedback session, and not a firing session, that day in Dayton. It was well worth the risk!

Feedback can best be viewed as a gift. We can give it and we can receive it. In either case it should have a positive effect on both the giver and the receiver.

This is Bowling?

M. Scott Myers was one of the most innovative and influential industrial/organizational psychologists of the twentieth century. His classic 1970 book, *Every Employee a Manager*, details the application of his work at Texas Instruments. Myers did a lot of consulting and one of the examples he used regarding the need for feedback was the game of bowling. He would show a visual depicting a bowler rolling his ball toward the ten pins at the end of the alley. Then he would overlay a curtain between the bowler and the ten pins. So, when the ball hit the pins, the bowler had no idea how many had been knocked down! Bowling from behind a curtain would not be much fun. Playing the leadership game without feedback is like bowling with a curtain stretched across the alley. It wouldn't be any fun either.

The Perfect Gift: Give Constructive Feedback

Constructive feedback should be viewed as a gift, the perfect gift, for the aspiring leader and for the dedicated, hard-working follower. If we think of it as a gift, and it is, it will be easier to deliver. In fact, if "you," (remember this is an alternate shot hole) are not in the habit of delivering constructive feedback at every opportunity, or looking to receive it on a regular basis, you've got to get with it. There's a lot of joy in giving gifts and in receiving them as well.

You have probably been exposed to recommended approaches to giving constructive feedback. You may have your own process and find it works well for you. That's great! If you don't have one, or don't think you do it well, or want to check your process, here are steps I recommend.

■ *Step One. Tell the person involved the constructive purpose(s) of the feedback.* In preparation, ask yourself, "Am I sure about my information, facts, observations, perceptions, etc.?" It may help to write down the constructive purpose(s) as an aid to ensuring validity. The road to improvement begins here.

■ *Step Two. Describe your observations in very specific, objective terms.* Get to the point. Don't beat around the bush.

■ *Step Three. State your reactions to what you observed.* Use "I" statements to let the person know your thoughts and feelings about the observations.

■ *Step Four. Now, let the person respond.* This may be the hardest part for you. You've stated the situation in steps one to three. Now ask for the person's reactions, thoughts, etc. You need to begin the dialogue, which will lead to the opportunity for improvement.

■ *Step Five. Work together to develop specific suggestions for improvement.* Help the person to think through ways in which improvement can be achieved. Be willing to go along with their ideas if they make sense and could work, even if it is not the way you would do it. If they lack the experience to come up with suggested actions, or if they just can't, or if in the less probable instance they won't, be prepared to provide direction.

■ *Step Six. Summarize the person's agreed upon action plan and pledge your help and support.* Yes, a pledge, a promise, not just an expression of support. Remember, as leader you are heavily invested in the success of all your people. Your success depends on it.

Here are three other suggestions regarding the feedback process. First, if you cannot think of a constructive purpose for giving the feedback you are considering then *do not give it at all!*

Second, one way to avoid the common fault in Step Two above, i.e., not getting to the point, is to complete your comments relating to Steps One, Two, and Three in *sixty seconds or less.* Practice in advance if you think you'll have difficulty doing this. The time spent in practice will be paid back in the feedback session. Look at this as being like the 10-second rule regarding putts, which Meg Mallon (hole #3) well remembers.

And third, as you engage in the feedback discussion, follow the communication tactic the very skilled leader uses consistently in all conversations: *Listen, listen, listen!* Listen to what is said. Listen to what the person may be trying to say. Listen to silence. And when all your listening is done, ask one more question!

It is wise to share this feedback process with your people. It is not magic. It is not a secret leadership technique. It's pretty much simple logic and common sense. Share it with all the folks in your 360-degree sphere of influence. Then all can help make constructive feedback an easy gift to give.

People want feedback. It is natural to ask, "How am I doing?" It is true of professional golfers with their volumes of statistics. It is why we put speedometers in automobiles, altimeters in airplanes, scales at weight-watchers, and insist on report cards for our school children. In all games and sports activities the participants want to know the score. Performance feedback must be accurate and timely. It serves as a reward when people, teams, or organizations do well. It leads to plans for improvement where it is needed. It also tells people someone cares how they are doing and that what they do is important.

By the Numbers

The management of a large manufacturing unit was concerned about increasing production and quality problems. They determined that the cause was a high level of both tardiness and absenteeism. Supervisory efforts to get people to show up for work were largely ineffective. Punishing tardy employees caused them to not come to work at all if they were going to be late. They would rather turn around and go home than be punished.

A young supervisor, recently returned from "charm school" (a leadership class), asked his boss if he could try using a basic feedback technique he had learned in class to reduce the absences. The boss said yes, with the usual caveat, you can't spend any money.

The supervisor obtained some large sheets of chart paper. He began to write two numbers on a chart taped to a support column in his department. Each day the numbers changed. He said nothing to the employees about the chart.

After a few days, an employee asked what the numbers meant. The supervisor told him that one was the number of good parts produced in the department the previous day and the other the number of employees who showed up on time that day.

Word about what the numbers meant soon got around the department. Employees were seen checking the chart. One employee observed, "Look, when more people are on time for work our production and quality numbers go up." Soon it became a game for the employees. They encouraged one another to be on time so they could see if they could continue to make the production and quality numbers go up.

In a few weeks, employees in the next department asked to post their information. Soon all the departments had posted their performance feedback charts and enjoyed competing with each other to see who could perform the best.

The young supervisor had removed the "curtain across the

bowling alley." The employees were now able to measure their performance. They saw themselves as full participants in the game and it resulted in improved performance.

Receiving the Perfect Gift: Constructive Feedback

The employees in the above example responded very positively to being given simple feedback. In other situations, the feedback process can be much more involved. Here are some thoughts regarding how to receive feedback for "you" (yes, in both your roles on this alternate play hole):

1. Adopt the mindset that you have something to learn from the feedback.

2. Relax, take a deep breath, try to think clearly.

3. Listen. Make sure you understand the feedback. Determine exactly what is being communicated to you. Ask for clarification if needed.

4. Do not respond if you feel reactive or defensive. Offer to get back together for discussion later. (This is very important. Don't jump into discussion if you are not calm, cool, and collected.)

5. Do respond in a way that communicates respect and admiration for the person who is giving you the gift of constructive feedback. Join with the other person in a discussion as to how the feedback can cause you to improve your performance.

Who Helps Leaders?

Skilled golf coaches, such as Butch Harmon and David Leadbetter, are able to help professional and amateur golfers through observation, feedback, and specific suggestions. The golfer must then translate the suggestions into action. This is the process of "continuous improvement" that drives all avid golfers. Unfortunately, though untold amounts of time and money are spent in business, industry, education, health care, and government on the continuous improvement of processes, comparatively little emphasis is placed on the continuous improvement of the leaders of the people on the front line.

Who helps leaders in today's organizations identify their fundamental leadership skill deficiencies? Sadly, there is not much help available beyond descriptions of leadership style and/or personality. These are nice to know, or to have confirmed, and they can be helpful. However, they are not a substitute for leadership effectiveness feedback, which identifies how leaders are doing as perceived by those whom they impact as leaders.

Performance evaluation, or performance appraisal, is advertised in most organizations as an annual process designed among other things as the tool for leadership effectiveness measurement. This annual "feedback requirement" is not viewed as productive by most employees and is a dreaded Human Resource Department obligation forced on supervisors and managers, who for the most part are ill prepared to do it and thus do it poorly. When it is done well it involves a leader/follower relationship that has been built on a day-to-day, situation-to-situation constructive feedback relationship, and which requires no more than a summary review at the time of the mandatory evaluation. In other words, the process should be a natural part of the way in which we successfully lead the organization.

A golfer hits a bad shot. The ball goes into the trees, in the water, out of bounds; the ball is topped and goes nowhere; or the ball is missed entirely, an embarrassing "whiff." The golfer's playing partners do not applaud, congratulate or say "that was a good shot." In the case of a "whiff", the "Tuesday Group's" members—gentlemen through and through—have been known to comment on the quality of their partner's practice swing! But that's the exception, golfers do not reward poor play. They don't demean it. They are just quiet about it. You struggle on your own. If you ask for help, they'll give it if they can. In the end, poor play is not overlooked. Your scorecard will tell the story. This golfing etiquette of not giving another golfer advice unless it is requested also applies to our giving feedback to peers and volunteers. The first step in such situations should be to consider whether the other person would like some feedback

What Is Your Leadership Score?

In organization life, poor leadership play is in my experience too often overlooked. People are told they are doing okay when they are not. We either don't like to deliver constructive feedback, don't understand our responsibility to the organization and its hard-working, contributing members, or are more concerned about someone's self-esteem than their job performance. Yet it is their job performance for which they are paid. Then one day we are faced with the person who has the security of twenty years on the job and literally refuses to meet our performance expectations. Why not?! He or she has been taught that mediocre performance is acceptable. And the organization develops the "M"—for mediocrity—disease.

What is needed is the application of the concept of "performance improvement for everyone" to the leadership development process in organizations. What needs to be done is to brush away the fuzz, the fluff, the political correctness, the "get a powerful mentor" behavior, etc., and get down to basics. Everyone should have a "Performance Improvement Plan" with clearly established performance expectations, which are used to determine whether the plan is being met. This will require regularly scheduled reviews and the opportunity for unscheduled reviews as necessary. It will require leaders to be coaches—what should be, but rarely is, their number one priority. It will provide the genuine gift of constructive feedback to organizational members. It will model the power of constructive feedback present in the game of golf and enhance the opportunity to significantly improve the effectiveness of organizational leadership just as application of feedback in the game of golf can lead to lower scores.

When the golfer strikes the golf ball, and a "slice" or a "hook" or "straight down the middle" follows, the result is clearly observable and measurable. When a follower knows what is expected, knows what the measurements are, and acts, the results will also be clearly observable and measurable. Timely, honest, specific, and constructive feedback is the "perfect gift for the aspiring leader." You can't hold a "slight edge" without it.

Which one of "you"—leader or follower—contributed the best shots on our "alternate shot" hole? What strengths did you observe? What areas did you identify for improving the giving and receiving of constructive feedback?

The next two holes, #15 and #16, will continue to build on how we can become better, more effective leaders and at the same time help our people maximize their ability to perform.

> *Leaders who are strong ask for help. Leaders who give more receive more.*[2]
>
> Dr. Edward Dwyer

Quick Tips for Improving Your Leadership Game

Real leaders typically understand and model the following in their day-to-day actions:

- Establish a climate wherein your ideas can be questioned or challenged by all your associates.

- Give positive feedback before giving negative feedback. Recognition of accomplishments makes the need for improvement easier to accept.

- NEVER, NEVER "kill the messenger."

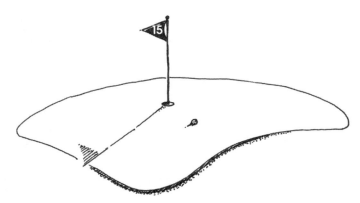

Accept Change: Adapt

I love golf. Every day's a different day. Every shot's a different shot.

Greg Norman, CBS *60 Minutes*, April 6, 1997

The game of golf is hundreds of years old. The game of leadership is older. Both have changed considerably over the centuries. Yet their essential elements remain.

Throughout history there have been games played with a ball and a club, or reasonable facsimiles thereof. The golf ball has changed considerably over time. The "feathery," followed by the "rubber guttie," then the "rubber core," and now a choice of two- or three-piece balls with solid or soft centers, have been the major developments. Clubs also have changed. Shafts were made of wood, usually hickory, for years. The first seamless steel shafts were introduced in 1912, the first metal-headed driver in the 1890s. These innovations were followed by matched sets of clubs. Now we have graphite shafts and space-age titanium club heads.

Improvements in golf equipment have made it easier for millions to play the game.

The leadership game has also changed over centuries. The industrial revolution, the great depression, two world wars, space and information technology, and social change have caused organizational restructuring in the drive to compete. Organizations still have hierarchies but also networks, autocratic leadership is giving way to inspirational approaches, homogeneous work forces are now culturally diverse, domestic markets have expanded to global markets, work done by individuals is now assigned to teams, and so on. These changes have greatly affected the way leaders are able to play the leadership game.

The leader's challenge is not unlike what the golfer faces in playing on a new, and therefore unfamiliar, golf course. The golfer must adapt to the new course requirements in order to be successful. The leader will continue to see changes in the leadership course and must be able to adapt if leadership effectiveness is to be maintained.

Adapt Now: Improve for the Future

A firm that manufactured large generating systems devised a superior diesel engine. It revolutionized the industry and captured most of the market. The company devoted all its resources to the production and sale of the engine. It was so efficient and reliable and had such wide customer acceptance that they sold all they could produce. This success continued for nearly twenty years.

Finally, and inevitably, a competitor developed a superior engine. They began to take market share away from the industry leader, who responded by commissioning its engineering department to develop a new engine. They got no results. Their engineers did not have the experience or capability to design and develop a new engine. After all, they had the world's best engine and had never given thought to having to design a better one. They could not adapt to their new circumstances!

The firm's solution was to improve their engineering staff's capability for the future. The engineering planning process was adapted to include initiating a new engine design and development project every five years. These projects were not focused on the need for a new engine but on the need to improve the capability to design one. The company went back to the basics, as we discussed on hole #6. Management focused on the situation: The issue of "engineering staff capability" was placed front and center. The necessary steps were taken to build a competitive design and development group. Poorly focused leadership had gotten them in trouble. Properly focused leadership was going to get them back on track.

No Prize for Coming in Second

An office-supply company periodically ran sales contests to "motivate" its salespeople. The same two people consistently won the contests and took home the prizes. Company management eventually recognized that the rest of the sales force did little better during the contests than they did in normal circumstances. Management's assessment was that "those people just aren't motivated."

The nonwinners, when asked, said they gave up competing because they knew they couldn't beat the two staff superstars, "there are no rewards for second place."

The inevitable management consultant was called in to look at the "motivation" problem. After some discussion and analysis, the consultant suggested some changes in the scoring of the contests. In addition to overall winners, awards should go to those who improved their individual performance numbers by the highest percentage. In that way, the salespeople would be competing against themselves (just like in golf) and not against the superstars.

The adaptation of the contest rules resulted in staff members significantly improving their individual productivity. They were challenged in a positive way. The organization experienced a future of increased sales.

Some Adapt, Some Don't

There seem to be some consistent differences between the results of first and second shift operations in production facilities. The second shift tends to out-perform the first. The second shift personnel are usually younger and have fewer years of service than the first.

For example, the second shift of a warehousing operation developed a new way to feed large parts down the line. They replaced an expensive method of operating a conveyor belt with a simple gravity feed system. Management was pleased with this continuous improvement effort by the workers and presented the idea to the first shift crew. The people on days wouldn't buy the idea. It wasn't theirs—a good example of the "not invented here" syndrome. They were not going to adapt.

So, the conveyor belt ran on the first shift and, after the millwrights took a half-hour to change it, the gravity feed system ran on the second. This continued for six months until management went ahead and instituted the gravity feed for both shifts. Thus a good idea developed by a group of workers to improve operations was delayed from full implementation for six months because another group of workers and a less than forceful management team refused to adapt to the change.

The late Dr. Norman R. F. Maier, professor of psychology for many years at the University of Michigan, taught his quality/acceptance theory of decision making at the university and as an international consultant to numerous organizations. His theory, in summary, holds that a decision consists of two parts: quality and acceptance. Quality refers to the objective value of the decision, i.e., is it substantively the best choice. Acceptance refers to the willingness of those affected by the decision to accept it. Obviously the best match is high quality and high acceptance. The second shift operation made their decision based on the high quality and high acceptance of the "gravity feed system over the conveyor belt" in our example. When the high quality decision was met by the low acceptance of the first shift, the change was not accepted.

The other decision option involves low quality and high acceptance. This is the option the first shift decided upon and continued with until many months later when the "gravity feed system" was put in place on both shifts. The example illustrates Dr. Maier's point concerning the importance of both acceptance and quality in the decision-making process, and their impact on implementation of a decision. Acceptance by those affected can overcome some deficiencies in quality, but quality will not overcome deficiencies in acceptance. This is an important concept for the leader to remember, and consider, especially when attempting to implement organizational change.

What? Me, Adapt?!

Groups and teams have difficulty accepting and adapting to change. Individuals also have a hard time doing what the outsider looking in sees as the obvious action. A greenskeeper once told me what he called his favorite golf story. He actually saw this happen.

A foursome teed off on a 420-yard par-four, dogleg left, with water bordering the dogleg. The hole had just been lengthened from its former 395-yard length by moving the tee back. You could play the fairway, or if confident of a 200-yard drive in the air, go over the water to cut the dogleg for an easy second shot. That was before the tee change; now it was at least 220 yards to cross the water. The first three players hit their drives comfortably down the fairway. The fourth, let's call him Charlie, lined up to cut the dogleg. It's the way he had always played this hole. His tee shot landed in the water ten yards short of the fairway.

His partners assumed Charlie would take a drop at the point at which his ball began to cross the water. Not so, apparently undaunted Charlie teed up another ball and with a mighty swing launched the ball once again over the water. Splash! Now certain he would take a drop, his partners picked up their bags and started to walk off the tee. But not Charlie. He proceeded to hit a third, fourth, fifth, sixth and finally a seventh shot. Seven balls in the water! All the while, his playing partners are saying, ``Take a drop, let's go.''

Charlie slammed his driver in his bag and without a word headed in the direction of where his last ball had crossed the water. His partners headed down the fairway. To their amazement, when Charlie reached the water, he took his bag of clubs and pitched it as far as he could out into the pond. He watched it sink, and without a word, or a wave, headed for the parking lot.

Charlie's buddies did what real golfers do under such circumstances. They played on. As they putted out on the green, they saw Charlie heading back to where he had thrown the clubs in the water.

Charlie strode to the water's edge and, without breaking stride, into the water. Didn't take off his shoes or roll his pant legs up. He was obviously trying to spot his bag. Then he reached down and pulled the bag out of the water. His partners cheered and applauded as the bag broke the water.

Charlie held the bag in the air. He unzipped a pocket, reached in, pulled something out, and stuck it in his pant's pocket. He lifted the golf bag over his head and once again threw it out into the pond. Charlie turned, walked out of the water, and headed back to the parking lot.

Golfers can be frustrated by new tee locations, tree plantings, poor sand-trap maintenance, aerated greens, and so on, but most adapt. They don't let themselves become victims of the changes. Leaders can be frustrated too by the pace of change on the Global Leadership Course. There is a lot happening around them over which they have no control. The game is more difficult, complex, and competitive. You know, the last time you played the hole you could hit it over the water!

To be sure, Charlie lost control. He let his frustration overcome him. He lost the ability to laugh at himself. He just plain failed to learn from his repeated missed shots. Fortunately, he was able to retrieve his car keys!

You cannot afford to be a victim of change. You cannot throw away the keys to survival in the global marketplace. In fact your best defense against the inevitability of change is to go on offense, that is learning to welcome change, seeking it out, being an advocate of continuous improvement, and enjoying the challenge change brings. Your positive example will influence your followers and help them to effectively deal with change.

SARAH

The difficulty is not so much that change occurs. It is that many individuals have difficulty in accepting and adapting to it, as with the gravity feed system or a new tee location. People need help in adapting to new circumstances. Changes run the gamut from the very minor one, hardly even a blip on one's radar screen, to the significantly major ones that alter lives forever. In each and every case, people react to change in a predictable sequence. It is important for the leader to understand this sequence and to recognize that it applies to all change from the most insignificant to the most dramatic. It is even more important that leaders help those in their sphere of influence adapt to necessary change. The sequence of emotional reaction to change is identified by the acronym SARAH.

When Ann and I concluded that she was indeed pregnant with Kevin after five children, and nine years since the birth of Lisa, the youngest, we went into SHOCK. We both expressed some ANGER that our settled family situation was about to change. Of course we commiserated with each other and offered up the typical, "this cannot be happening to us." In other words we went into REJECTION. As we worked on this "significant change" to our family life, we got help from the rest of the family. Ann began by telling each of the children that we were going to experience a blessed event. Mark, the oldest at 17, was first. His reaction was one of surprise but very positive. The others—Tim, Kathy, Dave, and Lisa—jumped on board as well in word and action. Kathy and Lisa went with Ann on visits to the obstetrician. Mark subbed for me at Lamaze class when I was out of town, and Tim served as the "family sitter" when needed.

In short, everyone was involved and ACCEPTANCE of our family change went well.

Others use the SARA—without the "H"—acronym to explain the change process. Note that I refer to it as the biblical SARAH, after our granddaughter, Sarah. And the reason is important. Let me explain.

People naturally react to change in the manner described by the SARA sequence. You should expect that they will. You need to exercise emotional restraint and allow them to express Shock, Anger, and Rejection on the way to Acceptance. Then, and this is so important, as leader you must provide individuals the "H" in SARAH, and that is HOPE. Hope in a future that will be better than the present. Kevin gave that to our family in many ways. We experienced SARAH and we adapted.

Golf: Thy Name Is Adapt

Golfers cannot be afraid of change. On the contrary, golf is a game where the very best players engage in never-ending self-criticism, self-reflection, and self-correction. They are also constantly adapting to changes in courses, conditions, equipment, or physical capacity. The best golfers spend a lot of time looking at themselves in the mirror to check their swings. They may even have invented the notion of continuous improvement. They provide the model for the leader who must adapt in times of change.

As mentioned when we played #8, Tiger Woods continuously seeks to further perfect his golf swing. Tiger won the 1997 Masters Tournament by 12 strokes and a record low score of 270. After celebrating the win, he looked for any flaw in his swing and saw about ten! He then took a year to overhaul his swing and in another two years "played by far the best golf of my life." The golf swing is always a work in progress, requiring adaptation and continuous improvement to be the best it can be.

Leaders need to demonstrate the willingness to adapt and improve their leadership skills, just as the golfer regularly checks golf swing mechanics. In addition to providing and receiving feedback, as discussed on hole #14, you should make the deliberate effort to seek it out. Such effort can lead to improving organization processes, follower success, and your personal leadership success. For help, consult with leaders whom you respect. Talk with leaders who have a style different from yours and are successful. Seek out those who want you to succeed and get their perceptions. And finally, discuss your leadership with people who have observed you in a variety of assignments over an extended period of time. Listen, and hear what they have to say. Consider their inputs. You'll be reinforced in your leadership effort and have ideas to consider for the adaptation and improvement of your leadership swing!

Dead Horses Can't Run

Our mission statement for the continuing education division at The University of Toledo was "quality education for quality performance." If only leaders spent as much time as golfers in this quest they would probably follow traditional wisdom, which says that when you discover you are riding a dead horse, the best strategy is to dismount! However, the general lack of concern for developing leadership effectiveness within organizations—because "we simply don't have the time or money to spend on "soft skills"—leads organizations to try these and other excerpts from the anonymously penned "Other Strategies with Dead Horses."

1. Buy a bigger whip.
2. Change riders.
3. Say things like "this is the way we have always ridden this horse."

4. Appoint a committee to study the horse.

5. Increase the standards for riding dead horses.

6. Appoint a team to revive the dead horse.

7. Create a training session to increase our riding ability.

8. Compare the state of dead horses in today's environment.

9. Change the requirements by declaring "this horse is not dead."

10. Hire consultants to ride the dead horse.

11. Harness several dead horses together for increased speed.

12. Promote the dead horse to a senior management position.

The difference between those organizations that make it in the "new realities of global organizational life" and those that don't is the cultivation of leaders with the ability to facilitate transitions: their own, the organization's, and those of their fellow employees. These leaders have the ability to adapt to new or modified surroundings in the same way the golfer adapts to a swing change, a new golf course, or changes in the weather.

As a leader, you also need to be proactive. Tiger Woods changed his golf game after winning the Masters, causing people to wonder, "what's he doing?" You need to be careful of "if it ain't broke there's no need to fix it," just as our diesel engine firm learned. They needed an "oil change" and didn't recognize it because everything was running so smoothly.

Today's organizations need leaders who can make change happen. Such leaders are the focus of this book. You, the leader of people, can do the job. You have to be focused, flexible, and adaptable. You need to understand and deal with the effects of SARAH when change occurs. You need to be a realistic decision maker who understands that people have to accept decisions in order for them to really work. You are motivated by results just as the golfer is, and you are dedicated to playing the Global Leadership Course in par or better. Like all of us, you'll need help along the way.

*Even if you are on the right track, you'll get run over if
you just sit there.*

Will Rogers, humorist

Quick Tips for Improving Your Leadership Game

Real leaders typically understand and model the following in their
day-to-day actions:

- See adversity, bad bounces, and landing in divots as challenges to overcome.
- In times of change be very proactive in communicating to your people and dispel false rumors.
- Reward innovative efforts aimed at continuous improvement, even when they don't work out well. Edison failed innumerable times before succeeding.

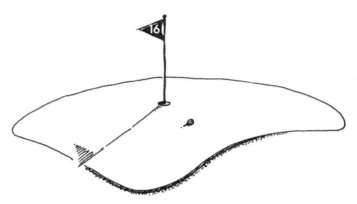

Caddies, Coaches,
and Teams

Life is tough but it's tougher if you're stupid.

John Wayne

"Stupid" is defined in *Webster's New World Dictionary and The-saurus* as being "senseless, brainless, shallow, imprudent, illogical, foolish, irresponsible, misguided, narrow-minded, irrational, and unintelligent" and with other not so complimentary descriptors. Stupid leaders are those who do not realize the value and contri-butions of the caddie, the coach, and the team!

Here's something to think about:

1. Name the five wealthiest people in the world.
2. Name the last three winners of the Miss America contest.
3. Name five people who have won either a Nobel or Pulitzer prize.

4. Name the last five mayors of your town.

5. Name the last three Oscar winners for best supporting actor or actress.

6. Name the World Series winners of the past decade.

How did you do? I did terribly! The point is, fame is fleeting and we don't pay much attention to the headliners of yesterday. We're talking about the best in their fields or competitions. They fade away rather quickly.

Here's another quiz. See how you do on this one.

1. Name three friends who have helped you through a difficult time.

2. Name a few people who have made you feel appreciated and special.

3. Name the five best teachers you've had in school or in your organization life.

4. Name the three best bosses you've worked with.

5. Name five people you enjoy spending time with.

6. Name the group of people with whom you have accomplished the most.

Easier than the first quiz? For your sake, I certainly hope so. And the lesson is? The people who make a real difference to us, and for us, are not the famous, the wealthy, or the award winners. The ones who mean the most, the ones we have little difficulty in remembering, the ones we never forget, are the ones who care about us. The Global Leadership Course is a tough one to play, and as a leader you have to go out and play it every day. You shouldn't play it alone. In fact, if you try to play it without the support of caddies, coaches, and teams of followers you will not succeed. You'll also need to be a caddie, a coach, and a team member.

Lead and Help, Help and Lead

On this hole we're going to look at the help we get in leading and the help we need to give as leaders. Here are some annotated definitions, with apologies to *Webster's New World Dictionary and Thesaurus*, to keep in mind as we discuss caddies, coaches, and teams.

■ *Caddie.* One who attends a golfer [leader], carrying the clubs [providing help and support, doing the heavy lifting].

■ *Coach.* An instructor or trainer [i.e., a vehicle to transport very important persons from where they are to where they want to be].

■ *Team.* Two or more horses [a workgroup] harnessed to the same plow [goals and expectations] in cooperative activity.

Caddies First

Let's begin with the origin of caddies. Piecing together history and golf legend, here's a story. Mary, Queen of Scots, lived in France as a young girl for her education and protection. Her father, King James IV of Scotland, was an enthusiastic golfer. Mary inherited his love of the game and, while in France from 1548 to 1558, went to school and played golf for enjoyment. She was properly chaperoned as she played and was guarded by cadets from a military school hired for the purpose. Mary liked this a lot, and when she returned to Scotland (not a very good idea for her in the long run) she took the practice with her. In French, the word "cadet" is pronounced "ca-day" and the Scots changed it to "caddie." Adopting French terms was not unusual for the Scots. If you have a better story let me know.

Each of you could develop an extensive list of people who have "caddied" for you over the years. The list would include relatives, friends, teachers, associates, bosses, and so on. The list should probably include all those whom you have followed, either because they were in authority, or because you were motivated to do so. All have influenced you in some way. If I were to ask you to list these people—especially your past bosses whom you served for a sufficient amount of time—you could do it.

I wager you could also describe them in a very few words, like one or two. For example, my first boss was in the nursery/landscaping business. I worked for him during summer vacation when I was 16. He was "dishonest." My last formal boss was "gutless." In between, lest you feel sorry for me or think I caused their poor leadership behavior, I was fortunate to have some very good leaders as caddies and coaches. Develop your own list. You'll have fun doing it. It will tell you a lot about who you are and how you got there.

Praise for Scottish Caddies

My friend, Mike Maggiano, and his golfing buddies went to the United Kingdom for golf and to attend the last two days of the 2003 British Open Championship. I called him after his return for a trip report. They had a great time. If you are a real golfer, you'd enjoy knowing, or enviously knowing, they played Troon, Turnberry, Carnoustie, Old and New St. Andrews, and a course I had not heard of, named Kings Barns. Mike described it as being hailed as the finest new golf course in the world. Must be something!

Mike commented on the Scottish caddies who helped him and his friends as they played these courses. In short, he said, "The caddies were great everywhere we played. They really helped us to achieve the greatest success we could within our skill levels." He said they demonstrated a confidence in their abilities as caddies that you don't see in the United States. "They kept us optimistic about our play," added Mike, "knowing we were nervous about playing such historic courses. On every course, the caddies were able to recognize our capabilities and then helped us to play within them. They added immeasurably to the fun we had playing."

How good a job do you do as a leader to "recognize (your people's) capabilities and then (help them) play within them?" How good a job does your leadership do in this regard?

Caddies Can Inspire

Our daughter, Kathy, managed the Inverness Country Club Pro Shop in 1986 and 1993. Inverness is a classic Donald Ross-designed golf course, which opened in 1903. As you know, it has hosted several championship tournaments, including the 2003 U.S. Senior Open. The first championship held at Inverness was the 1920 U.S. Open, which was the first Open for golfing legends Gene Sarazen and Bobby Jones. Byron Nelson, another legend of golf, was the head professional at Inverness from 1940 to 1945. *Golf Digest,* in its biannual course rankings for 2003–2004, rated Inverness the 17th best course in the country and the #1 course in the state of Ohio. Kathy was invited to manage the pro shop for the PGA Championship Tournaments of 1986 and 1993 by Master PGA Professional, Don Perne, who was then the Inverness head professional. She also had the opportunity to meet all of the top golfers of the time. She has her favorites but thought as a whole they were a great group of people.

During the l986 tournament practice rounds and tournament play, Kathy requested the professionals sign a commemorative 18th hole flag for her then 12-year-old brother, Kevin. The flag has the signatures of Arnold Palmer, Lee Trevino, Nick Faldo, Paul Azinger, Calvin Peete, Greg Norman, Bob Tway, and many more. She also had a second flag signed. These flags, long since framed, have hung on Kevin's walls in many states and countries. They helped begin his love for golf, in no small part due to the inspiration of his "first caddie" Kathy. Incidentally, the second flag reads, "To Kevin, Best of Luck. Jack Nicklaus."

Tom Watson and Bruce Edwards

Professional golfers and country club amateurs rely greatly on the assistance, counsel, and yes, inspiration of caddies as they play their games of golf. Caddies know the golf course. They can match the golfer with the golf club best suited for the shot at hand. The caddie knows the layout of the course and importantly knows the greens. The ability of the caddie to provide appropriate help can greatly influence the golfer's success.

One of golf's most sad but heartwarming stories of 2003 was that of Tom Watson and his relationship to Bruce Edwards, his caddie of thirty years. Watson dedicated his Senior British Open championship to Edwards, who is terminally ill with ALS, amyotrophic lateral sclerosis, or "Lou Gehrig's disease." Edwards, who has been called the "Arnold Palmer of caddies," was unable to caddie for Watson in England due to his illness. He returned to "Watson's bag," however, for the Champions Tour's final major tournament of the year, played in Aloha, Oregon. Fittingly, Watson won with a four-foot birdie putt on the final hole and commented, "I promised Bruce I was going to do it. I promised I was going to win for him."

Bruce Edwards as of this writing apparently plans to caddie for Watson as long his illness allows. Hopefully, the team will win many more tournaments. Ironically, Watson is now also serving as a caddie, or "helper," to his long-time teammate and friend. The "tables have turned" as they often do in supportive relationships. Watson with others formed the "Driving4Life" fund to raise monies for the research into a cure for ALS. He also reportedly contributes significantly to the care and treatment Bruce Edwards needs as he fights his illness. This is a situation where the golfer (caddie) hopefully helps the caddie's success.

There are many potential caddies in our midst who, if we are wise enough to turn to them, can, and will, greatly enhance the effectiveness of our leadership game.

Next, Coaches

I repeat, a "coach" is an instructor or trainer [i.e., a vehicle to transport very important persons from where they are to where they want to be].

The owner of a very successful printing company was asked to explain his approach to leadership. His answer emphasized the importance of having a good organizational team and the role of the leader in coaching that team. He said he learned a valuable leadership lesson from his high school counselor (caddie). She had a plaque on her desk that read, "Success occurs where preparation meets opportunity." He took the message to heart and practiced it through his approach to continuous learning both for himself and his employees. He provided skills training for employees' current jobs and educational opportunities for future challenges. He claimed, "My success and the success of those around me can be traced to that little plaque on my high school counselor's desk."

According to the ancient philosopher, Cicero, "Education is a person moving forward from cocksure ignorance to thoughtful uncertainty." Over the years, I have been frustrated by the "cocksure ignorance" (Cicero) or "stupidity" (John Wayne) of so-called leaders in all types of organizations, who place little value on the development of their leadership cadre. Millions of dollars and countless hours are spent on the latest management development fads, which invariably are a rehash of the obvious but come in appealing packages. The "programs of the month" are hailed in the board room and the training department, while the recipients shake their heads, roll their eyes, yet continue to try to do the best they can, suffering through the "new administrivia", and waiting for the next program.

Is Coaching a Priority?

The failing here is that the "program of the month" approach is based almost exclusively on "what" we want to accomplish, such as lean manufacturing, quality networks, re-engineering, reduced costs, and so on. These are all good concepts with desirable outcomes for the organization. The "how" of accomplishing these objectives is left to the abilities of the individual leaders in the organization. These leaders, responsible for leading their teams to the production of the organization's output, are the people who provide bottom-line product profitability. They are at the forward edge of the battle area in fighting the competition. They are the ones who need the support to get the job done. They need to know not only what is expected but also how results can be achieved. They need to be coached as leaders. Too many organizations do not view this as a high enough priority.

The leadership development of first- and second-level managers in organizations is not well-supported by the "leaders" in the immediate levels above them. They, by and large, do not ask for it, help in the design of it, or support participation in any such program. Perhaps it is because they are not encouraged to do so. Middle managers have been well trained in the importance of today and tomorrow, but not the day after tomorrow. They are under a lot of stress to see that things get done and therefore they tend to be doers, often assuming the responsibilities of their subordinates, rather than their primary leadership role of teacher and coach. And the reason, of course, is they have been taught to respond in this way by their leaders.

Another Short Self-Assessment

Back on #4 and #12, you had the opportunity to assess yourself on ethics and courage respectively. As we mentioned then, scorecards are integral to the game of golf. Keeping score is also integral to the game of leadership. I suggest you score yourself again, this time on some leadership skills associated with "coaching." Use Figure 16-1 as your scorecard. As with the "ethics" and "courage" self-assessments, use a forced distribution to score yourself by rank ordering the skills from 5 (most effective) to 1 (least effective). Your scoring will provide a measurement of relative effectiveness on these skills.

Once again, if you have scored yourself, it was probably difficult to work out the forced distribution. Hopefully, the process generated some thoughtful insight into your quest to be an effective coach.

Now, if you are interested, ask some others to rate you using the same forced distribution. Any difference between their percep-

FIGURE 16-1.
Sample leadership coaching assessment.

As a leader, I:

_____ Provide for individual job skills development.

_____ Provide appropriate help and support.

_____ Urge people to think independently.

_____ Provide timely feedback on performance.

_____ Teach others to be leaders.

Using a forced distribution, rank order the skills from 1 (least effective) to 5 (most effective), according to the following leadership effectiveness scale:

1—Least effective

2—Less effective

3—Acceptable

4—More effective

5—Most effective

SOURCE: Adaptive Leader Consulting Associates, Ltd., *Adaptive Leader Skills Assessment.* Copyright 1994.

tion of your coaching skill and your own evaluation is important to know and analyze.

Lessons for Coaches

Maybe you have been fortunate and had the benefit of good leadership coaching. If so, terrific; it will make your job as coach a lot easier. And you will understand its value.

There are lessons for good coaching in each of the holes we have played on the Global Leadership Course. Apply them as appropriate to yourself and to those you are teaching to lead. A former coach told me that coaching was a simple process provided one wants to be a coach. He said you need to assess talent, support strengths, strengthen weaknesses where necessary, know whom to push and whom not to push, and give a pat on the back when needed even if someone isn't doing well. First and foremost you need to know what motivates each performer and provide the right motivational environment.

Starfish

In Joel Barker's classic video, *The Power of Vision*, there is a scene in which a young man is walking a beach shortly after dawn. As he walks, he picks up starfish from the sand and tosses them out beyond the surf line. A man sees him doing this, and asks him, ``Why are you throwing the starfish back into the sea?''

He replies, ``If I don't they will die.''

``But,'' says his observer, ``there are so many, you can't possibly make a difference.''

The young man does not hesitate. He picks up another starfish and tosses it out to sea. Turning, he says, ``It made a difference for that one.''[1]

You owe it to those who follow you to make a difference for them. Often, and probably most impactful of all, the example of your actions, namely doing the right thing, results in those coaching moments that provide lifetime lessons to others.

Dear Mr. Stein

The following letter was read during the funeral services for Joseph B. Stein, father of our neighbor, Helene Helburn. Mr. Stein died December 13, 2001 at the age of 97. The letter is reprinted here with the kind permission of Helene Helburn and her mother.

September 5, 2000

Dear Mr. Stein,

You may not remember me, but I worked for you thirty years ago at the jewelry store. If you had not hired me to work for you I probably would never have been able to afford my tuition here at St. Francis (de Sales High School).

I was very pleased to see your letter to the editor in the Blade recently. You may not have realized it at the time, but you had a very positive influence on me. I was a shy, fourteen-year-old boy lacking much self-esteem. Every day after school I took the bus downtown to the ``clock in the middle of the block.''

You were patient and kind to me and trusted me to run those important errands. Once I dropped a whole tray of expensive watches and you calmly helped me pick them up and encouraged me to be more careful. I never forgot that. I thought I would be fired for sure!

Now I am a Catholic priest and work with young men who attend our school. I want you to know that you helped me to be the minister that I am today. Thank you for all that you did for me. I know that I wasn't the only student from our school you hired, and I am sure that there are many young men today who feel the same way that I do. I hope that I have the opportunity in my lifetime to make a similar positive impact upon as many people.

I hope and pray that you enjoy good health. My mother still proudly wears the jewelry that I bought her from your store.

God Bless,
James R. Sanford, O.S.F.S.

The Socratic Method

Socrates (470–399 B.C.), the famous Greek philosopher and teacher, was a well-known intellectual whose teaching and coaching methods endure today in what is known as the Socratic method. He taught, mentored, and coached, not by giving answers, but by questioning and causing his students to think and to engage in dialogue. Socrates was convinced the human mind could arrive at truth only through a process of questioning and discussion. He was, above all else, an incomparable questioner, an exceptional listener, and the model for leadership coaching. Hopefully your leaders practice the Socratic method with you, but even if they don't, you can practice it with those whom you lead.

Coaches can help improve your game of golf or your leadership game. Let the good ones help you. Mentors can help too, so long as they don't lead you to a career built on "sucking up." That doesn't work in golf, and anointed leaders who don't lead can trash organizations. In golf, only you get to swing your club. The same is true in leadership, where you must eventually, if not sooner, make your own decisions. And trust me, your followers are watching, and judging, how well you play the leadership game and whether or not you are hitting your own ball.

And Now Teams

I repeat, a "team" is two or more horses [a workgroup] harnessed to the same plow [goals and expectations] in cooperative activity. Over the past ten years, organizations seem to have discovered another panacea for organizational ills. It is the team concept.

Teams have been with us forever, as *Webster's* definition would seem to indicate. The good ones share in a collective goal, put their self-interests aside, enjoy and are rewarded by the synergy that results. Such teamwork is very hard to come by in the organizational setting. It certainly cannot be mandated.

Team Competition in Golf

Golf is an individual game; so is leadership. However, in golf, at the professional level, there are three exceptions of note. They are the Ryder Cup, the President's Cup, and the Solheim Cup. All are international team competitions that pit U.S. players against international ones. The Ryder Cup and President's Cup involve PGA players. The Solheim Cup is an LPGA event. The competitions are held every other year and generate a lot of worldwide interest.

The make-up of these teams interests me. The U.S. Ryder Cup team, and the others as well, consists of twelve players. The first ten are selected based on the points individual golfers accumulate for top-ten finishes in PGA Tour events. The other two team members are selected by the team captain. President's Cup selections are based on money earnings from PGA tournaments, and Solheim Cup participants are selected based on their LPGA Tour results the previous year. The international teams are also determined on the basis of measured recent performance. The "best of the best" make up these teams.

Ryder, President's, and Solheim teams compete in a match play format, where the golfers compete against each other, not against the course. Scores reflect the number of *holes* won with the fewest strokes rather than the total number of *strokes* taken. The teams compete in three ways:

■ *Foursomes.* Two teams of two golfers each compete in an alternate shot format. (Remember our husband and wife team who partnered in a couples alternate shot tourney on hole #14?)

■ *Four-Ball.* Two teams of two golfers each compete in a best-ball format. Each player plays his or her own ball and the best score of the two counts for the team.

■ *Singles.* One player competes against another in match play.

These international cup competitions are exciting to watch. They are rarely settled until well into the final day of play, and often the winner is decided by the outcome of the final match. The skills of the players as individuals and in their contributions to their teams are evident. They are the best of the best. These are high performance teams. There are other high performance teams that we have all observed in sports and in more serious endeavors like a hospital emergency room, the precision flying of the Navy's Blue Angels, or the danger of an oil fire-fighting crew. However, the best of the best do not always together make for high performance as a team. The best mix of talents needed, and the proper interpersonal chemistry of the team members, is what the leader should search out when using teams for task performance.

Scramble

Business, and other organizational, teams, in my opinion, do not match up to high performance teams. I'm sure there have been exceptions, but for the most part they don't match up and in fact may be dysfunctional. They bring to mind a golf activity enjoyed by many people working in a variety of organizations. It is the "golf scramble" outing.

Golf outings are held for many and varied reasons, such as business, marketing, charity, social, and so on. The mechanism of the "golf scramble" is used to level the playing field as much as possible between the skilled golfer and the golfing hacker. Participants are placed in teams of four players and generally follow these rules of play:

All four team members tee off on each hole. The team members decide which tee shot they like the best, pick up the other three balls, and all play their next shot from the selected position. This procedure is followed for all shots on the hole including putting. The first ball in the hole is the team score.

Sounds pretty good doesn't it? If you have one good golfer you should do well. But here's the hooker, each team must use at least one of each team member's tee shots on each nine, a minimum of two for 18, and be able to show on the scorecard where this was done. This could dull the performance of the good golfer or put an even heavier burden for quality performance on that individual. And of course you can have all the possibilities of combinations of good and not-so-good golfing teams. Guess what, the team with the best balance of good golfers will get the lowest score and win the scramble. We won't get into buying "mulligans" as a contribution to a local charity!

Too great a reliance on team-management of organizations

can result in the "M" disease, mediocrity. Teams are proud to pronounce they function on a consensus basis.

Well, some golfers just are better than others. Wouldn't you want your best golfers hitting as many shots as possible when you are scrambling for success in the global marketplace? I think so. And, don't you want the best leaders making the business decisions affecting the organization's future. Can you afford a consensus approach in situations that require the best of leadership? Margaret Thatcher, former prime minister of England, is reported to have said, "Consensus is the negation of leadership." One of the difficulties organizational leaders face when they are appointed to school boards, community organizations, and volunteer efforts is the "golf scramble" formulation of the leadership teams.

What About Teams?

So, what should you as a leader do about teams? Teams are a tool for effective leadership when the situation calls for a team approach based on bringing together the necessary talent to accomplish a clear performance expectation. Choose the team members wisely based on their ability and willingness to contribute to the team task, that is, leaving their ego at the door. Help them to work together to maximize their synergy. Reward the team effort and don't forget the individual pat on the back for contributors to the team's success. Just don't let them substitute for your good judgment and wisdom.

There is one "team" you should not lose sight of, and this team should be allowed to play together to the fullest extent with you the leader. They are the people who serve as your "caddies" (helpers) in the day-to-day challenges of leadership. Together with them you can win a lot of Ryder Cup-type "foursomes," "fourballs," and "singles." This is where dedication to your leadership role as "coach" will pay big dividends. One of those dividends will be that when success is achieved and accomplishments are applauded, you can stand up and say, "It was a *team* effort."

Sir Thomas More: "But Richard . . . Why not be a teacher? You'd be a fine teacher. Perhaps even a great one."
Richard Rich: "And if I was, who would know it?"
Sir Thomas: "You, your pupils, your friends, God. Not a bad public, that . . ."

Robert Bolt, *A Man for All Seasons*

Quick Tips for Improving Your Leadership Game

Real leaders typically understand and model the following in their day-to-day actions:

- "How can I help?" Encourage associates to come to you when they need advice, information, decisions, problem-solving assistance, or coaching.
- Ask what went wrong, not who did wrong.
- Allow people to learn from their mistakes.
- Meet with your associates individually to identify what you can do to help them be more effective in their jobs. You will need to know each person's level of experience, confidence, and ability. Some may need structure, direction, and guidance. Others may need encouragement, confidence building, or emotional support.

An Optimistic Outlook

Know your limits and stay loose.

Stan Moyer, The Tuesday Group

One of the positive aspects of the game of golf is that golfers know that regardless of their play on the last hole or in the last round, there is always a next hole or a next round. This sparks more than the intense, eager interest of enthusiasm. The golfer is inclined to hope, even expect, that the best will happen on the next hole, or in the next round.

The "Shark," Tway, and "Zinger"

In 1986, Greg Norman, the "Shark," led all four of the major tournaments—the Masters, U.S. Open, British Open, and PGA—entering the final round of play. He had never won a major tournament. He was optimistic about his chances as he entered play on the last day of each of the tournaments. It was an optimism based on his position on the leader board. That optimism was supported by his confidence in his playing ability.

His optimism was sorely tested in the PGA when Bob Tway holed out from a greenside bunker on the 18th and final hole of the tournament to defeat Norman. Norman didn't lose all four majors in 1986, nor did he lose his optimism about his ability to play and win. Greg Norman was the 1986 British Open Champion.

When Bob Tway hit out of the sand trap alongside the Inverness Country Club 18th green he was optimistic about hitting a good shot. He knew he could make it. He had the skill. He'd practiced and played hundreds, probably thousands, of similar shots. Did he think it *could* go in the cup? You bet. Did he think it *would* go in the cup? Probably not, but he knew if he got it close it had a chance of going in. And it did. Bob Tway had beaten Greg Norman for the 1986 PGA Championship. As he leaped within the bunker, and then outside it, enthusiasm reigned at the Inverness Club. I know, I was there.

Paul Azinger holed out of a greenside bunker, a la Bob Tway, on the 72nd hole of the 1993 Memorial Tournament to beat Corey Pavin and the late Payne Stewart. Later in the year he beat Greg Norman on the second hole of a sudden death playoff, once again at the Inverness Club, to win the 1993 PGA Championship. Azinger had his best year as a professional in 1993 and was optimistic about his chances for a continuation of success in 1994. In December 1993, however, he was diagnosed with a lymphoma in his right shoulder. He turned his optimism to the hope that he would overcome his illness and return to his career as a professional golfer. He did return and within a few years was once again playing with the best of them. He won the 2000 Sony Open in Hawaii.

Optimism Defined

Optimism, as defined in *Webster's New World Dictionary and Thesaurus*, is "the tendency to take the most hopeful view of matters, it is a belief in the essential goodness of the universe, it is the belief that good ultimately prevails over evil, it is the inclination to hope for the best, cheerfulness, hopefulness, confidence, assurance, encouragement, happiness, brightness, enthusiasm, good cheer, trust, calmness, elation, expectancy, and certainty." It is the opposite of gloom and despair. An optimistic attitude is essential to the golfing and personal success of a Norman, a Tway, and an Azinger.

Real golfers, and hackers like myself, are eternal optimists about their golf game. Today's round, until proven otherwise, is going to be my best ever. And if not today, tomorrow! We tend to take the most hopeful view of the future in the context of the reality of our individual golfing ability.

Real leaders are believers that good ultimately prevails over evil, that quality performance prevails over inferior performance. Like the golfer, they see the future with hope. They are optimistic, rarely pessimistic. They understand the reality that the past is past and the attainment of goals rests in the present and the future. They take a positive approach to their responsibilities. They know their outlook on life and leadership is one of the few things within their personal control. The minds of the golfer and the leader are characterized by "hope"—the realistic perception that there is a way to proceed, that there is a future, that there is a solution to whatever confronts them.

Remember Bill Niehous

Back on #7 I introduced you to Bill Niehous, a former leader in the Owens-Illinois Inc. organization. In the mid-1970s, Bill was General Manager of O-I's Venezuelan operations. A real leader, Bill faced an extraordinary physical and mental test of self when he was kidnapped by rebel forces on February 27, 1976 and held hostage for three years in the jungles of Venezuela. I asked Bill how he had survived this experience. He told me he was prepared to survive by the way in which he had lived and worked prior to being kidnapped. Bill attributes his survival to the following five factors:

1. *Faith and support,* developed over the years, had become a part of him. It included his personal network of family, friends, acquaintances, and religious beliefs. He knew with confidence that his personal network was working as hard as possible to obtain his release.

2. *Communication,* actually the ability to communicate, was always a strength of Bill's. He had worked hard to develop a high degree of fluency in Spanish, the language of his host country. So, he was able to speak with his captors and read in Spanish. He also kept a diary.

3. *Conditioned to social environments,* Bill was not exercised in the sense of push-ups and pull-ups, etc., but well experienced in a variety of social situations within community, business, church, volunteer, and recreational settings.

4. *Empathy for the feelings of others* allowed Bill to understand his captors. He didn't like them but felt he needed to comprehend why they were rebelling against their government. He learned to understand why they felt downtrodden and oppressed. This understanding helped him to maintain the attitude that his life was well worth living and helped him to keep moving forward.

5. *A continuing optimism* that he would be rescued made Bill set goals and objectives for when he returned home. He made plans that, as he described it, "allowed him to climb a ladder, not leap over a wall." Initially, the plans were in terms of time. Bill was kidnapped in February and expected that his ransom and release would be settled by Easter and he would be home in time to see his son graduate from high school in June. That date came and passed. He focused on other events, like birthdays, his and Donna's wedding anniversary, annual family vacations, Christmas. As each step on the ladder confirmed his survival to that point, he set another event he wanted to participate in and waited to be released in time for it.

Bill eventually escaped from his captors on June 29, 1979 and was fortunately rescued by some Venezuelan farmers who recognized him and brought him to the authorities. An Owens-Illinois plane had him back in the states in less than twenty-four hours.

Bill considers himself to be a fortunate person, never a celebrity. He sees himself as a survivor and continues to express appreciation for all the people who worked so hard in attempting to obtain his release. He is still impressed by people who tell him they are so glad he made it back. Bill continues to work on a variety of community efforts and to further develop the five factors he credits for helping him survive his kidnapping. His advice to leaders is "forget difficulty, move forward, be positive and optimistic." Bill also loves to golf, and his advice to golfers is the same, plus "swing hard."

How Are You Doing?

I stopped at a Boston Market about a year ago for a carryout dinner. As the server, a teenage young lady, prepared the food she asked, "How you doing?" The question was posed with all the sincerity of the employee instructional handbook. "Well", I said, "I'm terrific" She looked at me with a somewhat startled expression on her face. So I poured it on, telling her it was just as easy to say "I'm terrific" as to say "I'm okay," and it makes me feel good when I do it. Now she is really looking at me as if I have just arrived from outer space and perhaps she should call the manager for assistance. So, I give her one last volley about how it doesn't cost any more to be upbeat and positive than to be dull and boring and besides it was a lot more fun for everyone. As I left the restaurant she was still shaking her head.

About two months later, I revisited the same Boston market. I ordered my food and waited as the server began to prepare it. Midway between the chicken and new potatoes, the server stopped, looked me in the eyes, and said, "I'm terrific!" Who says the little positive things we do don't have impact. Shades of making, not missing, a short putt! Leaders, and we all have the potential to lead, have the power to influence others. Or as I prefer, we have the power to establish an environment that can help to motivate others. Real leaders do it in positive, optimistic ways in minor and major situations, knowing the greatest potential for payback and progress rests on their positive, optimistic behavior. And it is the simple things that we control that can pay big dividends. I like to ask leadership program participants how many of them make the effort to smile and greet everyone at the start of each business day. Regardless of how you may feel, you can positively influence others' approach to the day with this simple effort. You're in control and you'll feel better for it too.

Only One Umbrella

A small rural church was crowded with parishioners who had come to pray for rain. A severe drought was ruining farm crops throughout the county. The minister noted, however, that only one person, a little old lady, had brought an umbrella to the service! Optimism is a confident hopefulness.

"A Hundred Times"

Years ago, a gentleman by the name of Bob Wallace headed up the New Products area for Owens-Illinois Inc. Wallace was so optimistic by nature that he often forecast potential markets at a hundred times their true size. When describing Wallace's optimism, then O-I Chairman Ray Mulford once commented, "If I had a life threatening disease, I'd want Bob Wallace to tell me because he would make it sound so good." Optimism is cheerfulness and enthusiasm.

A Million Bucks

A corporation had the opportunity to broaden its market base through the acquisition of a small Pennsylvania company. The price was close to one million dollars. The division head whose operations would benefit from the acquisition was in favor of the purchase. When asked whether he could spare the people to manage and technically support the acquisition, he replied, yes, without a moment's hesitation. (Later, he said he didn't give his response a moment of reflection either.) The acquisition was made and it turned out to be a failure. The responsible division head commented, "Boy, was I wrong! I ended up blowing a million bucks because I didn't think the situation through. As the years have gone by the memory of that error has saved me from several much larger mistakes." Optimism must be grounded in reality.

Shackleton Gets My Vote

In what I believe to be the greatest survival story of all time, Sir Ernest Shackleton, the noted Irish explorer, in 1914 led his twenty-six-man crew of the *Endurance* on a two-year odyssey from being lost in the Antarctic to eventual return to the safety of civilization. The story of Shackleton and the crew of the *Endurance* should be must reading for all who aspire to leadership. Shackleton did many things to help his men maintain a positive and optimistic attitude regarding the eventuality of a safe return. Suffice to say he set the example for leaders faced with maintaining optimism in the most extreme circumstances. One of the diversions organized for the crew was "soccer on ice." I'm certain had Shackleton foreseen the virtually unbelievable fate of the *Endurance's* ill-fated journey, he would have brought along some golf clubs and played golf on the ice as well. Shackleton often said, "Optimism is true moral courage."

For the golfer who's had a bad day on the links, or the leader who doesn't see things going well, I recommend reading any of several accounts of the voyage of the *Endurance*. It will put your difficulties in perspective and deliver positive inspiration. As a Navy warrant officer was known to say whenever faced with yet another challenge to be dealt with, "Great, another opportunity to excel!"

What Are Your Alternatives?

Organizations want their employees to be enthusiastic about their work. Some companies promote the notion of employee enthusiasm. They want their people to be eager, interested participants in the organization. This is good. It is, however, only part of being optimistic. You, as a leader, and your followers need to be optimistic for your mental health and physical well-being. You should be, and hopefully are, enthusiastic about the work that you do. But you need more. Let me explain.

Imagine that Figure 17-1A is a large picture window, a large single pane of glass. Now, imagine someone throws a brick at the window and breaks it. The whole window is destroyed.

Now imagine another window. That window, as shown in Figure 17-1B, is the same size as the picture window, but rather than being a single pane of glass it consists of several, actually nine, separate panes. Is that brick still handy? Pick it up and throw it at this window. What happened? You probably broke a pane or

FIGURE 17-1.
A. Single pane window. B. Multipane window.

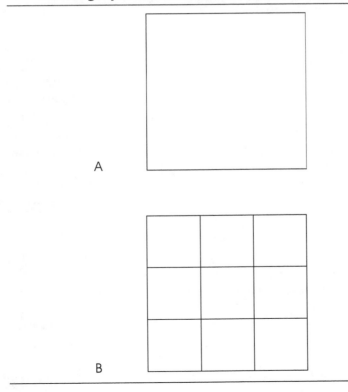

two, maybe even a few more than that, but you didn't break them all, and those remaining are still intact.

The windows represent life, your life. The single pane window is the person whose total existence is wrapped up in work. Destroy that existence through job elimination, firing, even retirement, and the person does not know where to turn. Nothing remains to be optimistic about. Their physical and mental health can be seriously affected.

On the other hand, the multipane window has panes remaining if the "work" pane is destroyed. As in Bill Niehous's case, there are other panes that can be relied on, such as family, friends, hobbies, and avocations. You need to make sure you have a multipane window for yourself, and as a leader you need to help your followers have multipane windows as well. You'll be a much better leader for it and your followers will be more effective. Optimism is about having alternatives.

"Stay Loose"

Stan Moyer, of the "know your limits and stay loose" quote introducing this chapter, is 88 years old. Since his retirement, Stan has played golf with a group of colleagues from the former Haughton Elevator Company, the original "Tuesday Group" first mentioned on hole # 4. Stan is a World War II veteran of the Battle of the Bulge. He spent his early professional life as a musician, playing with many of the greats of the "big band era." Stan has been a good golfer for years. Recently, true to his philosophy, he began limiting his play to six or seven holes, and he usually pars several of them.

I was introduced to Stan by Bob Lauer, a good friend and former vice president of engineering for Haughton. Bob asked me to join the group for one of their regular Tuesday morning outings. Subsequently, though most are quite a bit older, they asked the "kid" to join them on a regular basis. Stan's always effervescent behavior, his enthusiasm for telling jokes, and his joy in playing golf struck me from the start. So, one day I asked him to tell me what his philosophy of life was, as he so clearly enjoyed every minute of it. And he expressed his positive, optimistic approach to life succinctly, "know your limits and stay loose." Good advice for the golfer and the leader as well.

> *Instill optimism and self-confidence,*
> *but stay grounded in reality.*[1]
>
> Dennis N. T. Perkins

Quick Tips for Improving Your Leadership Game

Real leaders typically understand and model the following in their day-to-day actions:

- Expect things to turn out well! Build up your integrity and courage. Exercise optimism!
- Believe you can do it. Frank Stranahan, age 81, a great amateur golfer of years past, attended the U.S. Senior Open. In a television interview on Toledo's Channel 10 he was asked, "To what do you attribute your longevity?" His response, "Believing I can do it."
- Set an overall organizational tone of competence, integrity, and optimism. You can influence the spirit of everyone else. Be competent, optimistic, enthusiastic, and trustworthy, and a positive spirit will pervade your organization.

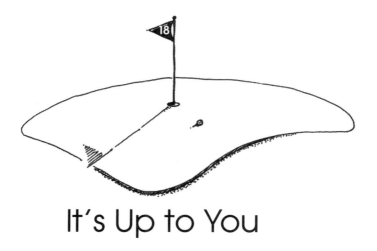

It's Up to You

Most dreams are attainable if the dreamer is ready to devote consistent, intelligent effort to them.[1]

Dr. Bob Rotella

One of the great things about golf is that the individual player is responsible, and accountable for his or her play. Golf is not a team game. It is an individual game. So is leadership! We have emphasized this throughout the round. You see, we don't want you to forget it. Also, we've been talking about you as a leader of people, not as a tactician, strategist, or technical person.

In golf, you alone are responsible for what happens to you. Whining is not allowed. Your ball ends up in a divot, goes into the water, sails out of bounds or takes a crazy bounce too bad. That's golf . . . that's life! So, too, leaders get into trouble. You can blame others, the economy, global warming, or whatever, but like the golfer you need to get over it and move on.

Don't Join the "They" Group

The most often expressed obstacle to effective leadership in my years of experience both as a leader and as a facilitator of leadership programs is "they." The infamous, slippery, unidentified "they" seems to be at the heart of the difficulty that first- and second-level managers have with being able to lead most effectively. Groups tell me, "if only 'they' would (fill in the blank), we'd be able to get the job done." I always encourage folks who have this difficulty to not inflict it on others when they move up the ladder and become "they." Many of these people are now "they" and their followers are attending leadership programs similar to ones they attended. And now, their followers are complaining about them as "they."

Golfers will try to improve on their game but rarely abandon what brings them success at the game. Jim Furyk has a golf swing like no other golfer but he learned to play with it; it works for him, as his 2003 U.S. Open Championship proves. I don't think he'll be changing it soon. Phil Mickleson is in a bit of a slump at this writing but I don't think he will change the left-handed swing he was taught in learning to play golf for the right-handedness of his baseball-throwing arm. Don't become part of the "they" group. Apply the lessons of Holes 1 through 17 now, and for the rest of your leadership career.

Focus on Quality and Customer Satisfaction

Small business success often results from a reputation for quality and a multitude of satisfied customers. When these businesses expand significantly, or are bought out by a larger company, the emphasis often shifts to profitability. Quality and customer satisfaction take a back seat as decisions concerning them are made at headquarters and not locally. The concept of developing employees to focus on quality and customer satisfaction as the key to profitability is often deleted from the equation.

A former colleague, who has consulted in the above situations, has asked managers to identify their major problem in expanding the business. An amazing 85 percent cite "managing people" as number one. When he asks how much management and leadership training do they provide, the answer is, not very much. What training they do provide is limited to processing paperwork.

A successful golf shot is always followed by a yet-to-be-taken, and evaluated, next shot. Success in business requires ensuring the continuation of the key elements of that success. You, as leader, are responsible for "managing people." You need to be sure that the elements of your organization's success are always a part of performance expectations and that your people are prepared and supported in their efforts to deliver them.

Opportunities Galore

Every golfing day is a new day. In fact, every hole, indeed every shot, is a new opportunity for success or failure. Success in golf requires that you erase the history of what you did yesterday, on the last hole, indeed on the last shot and focus on the next opportunity. In golf, the future always buries the past, the past does not bury the future. The best golfers spend a lot of time looking at themselves in the proverbial mirror, and on videotape, to check their swings. Self-reflection and self-criticism are common to the golfer. They are also common to the successful leader. Learn from your own leadership experiences by taking the time to analyze your successes and your failures.

Winning with a Team

In recent years, organizations have, I think, overemphasized the value of teams over the value of the individual. Individual initiative and creativity have been stifled in favor of often less substantial contributions of consensus-based team activity. That's okay if the objective is mediocrity! The obsession with teamwork aimed at symbolic cooperation and orchestrated as a "program of the month" has squelched the real source of energy ideas and, yes, leadership: the individual.

There have always been teams and teamwork in organizational life. The successful ones have strong leadership and responsible role players. They do not rely on forced relationships, diversity-based composition, or fabricated feelings of involvement and equal participation. They do rely on each member contributing substantively, following team leadership as appropriate, and taking leadership when the situation requires it. Successful teams appear to be seamless, each member at times acting as leader, at other times as follower. At all times leadership on the part of the individual is required. Teams are here to stay and therefore, you as leader, must deal with them, and deal effectively!

Teams can be effective, as we discussed while playing hole #16. I believe it is best to view your business team as you would a Ryder Cup team, or a baseball or football team. Each player has a responsibility to the team in the sense of being a good member. However, do not allow team member participation to anyone who does not have a specific and measurable responsibility. No one should be allowed to hide from the accountability for their contribution. Adopt this criterion and your team can be a winner! But I still agree with management guru Peter Drucker, who commented in a September 28, 1998 *Fortune* magazine interview, "Teams are the right strategy only for a very small number of situations."

Don't Fall to Fashion

A major problem you face is "fashion-conscious management." Organizations adopt and ask you to implement so-called revolutionary strategies, such as "down-sizing," right-sizing," "lean manufacturing," "just-in-time," "quality networks," and "re-engineering." These "programs" are bought and promulgated throughout the organization, usually at considerable expense in the dollars of time, currency, and disruption. They are proclaimed as the latest organizational panacea. Where they add to administrative and technical performance, great! Where they purport to make leading your people easier, beware!

Millions of words have been written about how to improve

one's golf game. Golfing gurus abound. Yet on-going, or recurring, failure stretches throughout the average golfer's life. Occasionally, golfers stumble on a "cure." The outcome is the euphoric state that overcomes the overly optimistic golfer. He or she now believes the ultimate path to lower scores has been uncovered. Drives are longer, iron play is better, and putts drop. But for most this is a false positive, a hallucination, and soon the despair of poor play looms again. The quest for the "great cure" begins again (new program, new club, new coach, new ball) and the cycle of elation, followed by failure, becomes a process that repeats itself . . . not unlike the lure of "fool's gold."

In reality, more than 90 percent of playing the game of golf or playing the game of leadership is fundamental and routine. The "gimmicks" may help for a while but they've all been tried before. Only the names have been changed to project an aura of discovery, innovation, and creativity. The dirty little secret is that the vast majority of followers are not fooled by this un-leader-like behavior. They know managers are "fashion-conscious" because they also know that most of what goes on in organizations is routine and boring. The secret to playing better golf is the same as the secret to more effective individual leadership: There is no secret! Don't fall for this stuff! If it's good, and on target, it'll fit right into your fundamental grip, stance, and swing.

Be Willing to Offer a Mulligan

The commanding officer of a nuclear submarine had a young petty officer second class arrested for a third DUI while the submarine was undergoing an overhaul in Mare Island, California. State law required a mandatory jail sentence for the third offense, and the young sailor was sentenced to one year in prison. Normally this would also result in discharge from the Navy. The commanding officer, however, had a hunch about the young man. So, he decided to try and give the young man a "mulligan." He went to the judge and bargained a reduced sentence with the sailor's leave time to be spent in jail plus a six-months restriction to the submarine. The young man was also reduced in rank and fined, but he got to take another swing at his Navy career. He became a model sailor, regained his original rating, and was eventually promoted to chief petty officer.

As a leader, you may not get a mulligan if you drive one into the rough. But, don't underestimate the power of a wisely used mulligan to give a second chance to one of your people. The mulligan can pay off big for both of you.

Don't Just Go Along to Get Along

Margaret Thatcher, the former prime minister of Great Britain, as we mentioned on #16, is reported to have commented, "Consensus is the negation of leadership." Leadership, the most valuable contribution a person can make to an organization, has been set aside by too many "managers" in the interest of cooperation, that is, getting along, instead of leadership in the pursuit of excellence. You need to be concerned about your approach to decisions. When acceptance of the group is critical, and the quality decision can come from them, consensus is a wise approach to deciding. However, at other times you must step up and be the decision maker, consensus or no. Your followers, and your organization, look to you to be courageous. The very nature of situational leadership requires that you be skillful in choosing the proper route to the decisions you face as leader. You need to be able to know when to consult your caddie(s) and when to just pick the club and step up and hit the ball.

Keep a Focus on the Day After Tomorrow

As we have emphasized during our round, "real leaders" take into account yesterday, today, and tomorrow, but they focus on the day after tomorrow! They know organizational survival depends upon excellence over time. Check the life span of companies in the *Fortune 500* and you will find most are relatively young. Few, if any others, span the nineteenth, twentieth, and twenty-first centuries, as does General Electric. Few companies today have had the type of leadership exemplified by Jack Welch during his tenure at GE. We need more "individuals" in our organizations, who focus on survival in the future while at the same time achieving results in the present. And they are needed everywhere.

Thumbnail Sketches

We need leaders who can be described as the following persons were in a company history written by a retired member of the organization.

■ Leader A is in my view, a terrific person. He is a man of good character and high intelligence. His activities and actions seemed to me to always be in tune with what he thought to be the best interests of the company.

■ Leader B is a tall, imposing man with very heavy eyebrows and handsome features. He is always immaculately and conservatively dressed. He expressed the feeling that his appearance sometimes kept people from getting close to him. Perhaps so, but he is a man well worth getting to know. He has exceptionally fine values and high moral standards. He is also, and not insignificantly, very competent.

■ Leader C is the best leader I ever met. He is very smart, a good motivator and a great coach. He has a warm and sincere interest in people. He is honest and straightforward. Although I knew some other leaders who got as good or maybe better results, C still gets my vote as #1.

■ Leader D is bright and politically skillful. She always supports her people and recognizes their good performance. She reads people extremely well and judges their capability accurately. She once told me she felt like the conductor of an orchestra. She liked to get each of her people to play their part well with good result for the group.

■ Leader E has good common sense and is smart and very hard working. He is one of my favorite business associates because he has integrity and high moral character. In no case, or situation, did I ever observe him exhibit anything but the highest level of integrity.

Pretty good commentaries about Leaders A, B. C, D, and E! What would your write-up look like today? How will people describe you and your leadership when you have completed your career? It's up to you.

Don't Settle for Less

"He has better flexibility than anybody. He works harder than anybody. He hits the ball farther than anybody. He putts better than anybody. And he wants to be the best player who ever lived. I think that pretty much explains it." (Tom Watson commenting on why Tiger Woods is the best golfer in the world as reported in *USA Today,* August 21, 2000.)

The yearning to play a better game of golf affects every golfer in the world. Everyone who is serious about the game is constantly striving, hoping, to improve his or her score. They may say, "I shoot in the 90s and that's good enough for me. I just like to play for the fun of it." This is a huge white lie and every golfer knows it!

Golfers first want to break 100, then desperately want to break 90. When the 90 barrier falls, the urge is to break 80, then to consistently shoot in the 70s; finally, par or better is the goal. Given the opportunity, the golfer will do everything possible to improve his or her golf game. The leader, enabled by the support of the organization, will do everything humanly possible to improve his or her leadership game. Real leaders, like real golfers, will not be satisfied with mediocrity for themselves or for others.

Don't Give In to the Cynics

I know what happens when participants return to the job after attending a leadership seminar or any "soft skill" management development activity. The boss says something like, "How was your vacation? Did you learn anything at "Charm School?" So, I counsel my participants to have at least a couple of suggestions for the boss, based on group discussions that can be of help to him or her and to the organization. You know, meet fire with fire, coach!

Do not be dissuaded by the pessimistic cynics who question your motives and actions, and those of others, to do the right thing. Cynics are certainly sometimes right in their views. They are also often not realistic in their thinking. Most assuredly they waste a lot of energy on their negative approach to life and leadership. Stay positive. You'll feel better and come out on top in the long run.

The 100th Monkey

Fact, fiction, or folklore, there is a story told of a young monkey living on an island with a colony of monkeys. Sweet potatoes, which grew on the island, were the staple food of the monkeys. The monkeys would scoop them up, covered with sand and dirt, and eat them. That is, except for this one female monkey. She would take her sweet potato to the water's edge and wash it off. Then she would eat it. Her siblings and others derided her, in monkey-talk of course, ``Why are you so foolish as to take the time to wash your sweet potato?'' And she would reply, ``It tastes better, that's why.''

Time went by, months and then years, and as the story goes the young monkey began to convince other monkeys of the wisdom of washing the sweet potatoes. First one, then ten, then fifty joined her. Now, for purposes of example, assume there were 300 monkeys on the island. The number of monkeys washing their sweet potatoes reached 99. The next day the 100th monkey, and all the other monkeys, began to wash their sweet potatoes!

The 100th monkey represents the concept of critical mass: Reach a certain point of action and you cannot stop the reaction from occurring throughout the mass. The concept of critical mass is fact and not a monkey story. It took a long time but our young monkey knew the proper way to eat a sweet potato. She stuck to her guns until she had carried the day with the other monkeys. It's up to you to exercise the same patience and positive attitude in seeing that the right things get done. Get critical mass on your side.

Will You Be the One?

My hope is that at least one of you becomes a more effective leader as a result of having played the 18 holes of the Global Leadership Course. If so, I will consider my work a success. It will only be a success for you if you are the one. It's up to you to identify and work on those ideas that will improve your leadership game. Just like the game of golf! Remember, in both the game of golf and the game of leadership, you must play your own ball. If you don't, you aren't golfing, and you certainly are not leading!

One evening an old Cherokee told his grandson about a battle that was going on inside himself. He said, "My son, it is between two wolves. One is evil: anger, envy, sorrow, regret, greed, arrogance, self-pity, guilt, resentment, inferiority, lies, false pride, superiority, and ego. The other is good: joy, peace, love, hope, serenity, humility, kindness, benevolence, empathy, generosity, truth, compassion, and faith."
The grandson thought about it for a minute and then asked his grandfather, "Which wolf wins?" The old Cherokee simply replied, "The one I feed."

Author Unknown

Quick Tips for Improving Your Leadership Game

Real leaders typically understand and model the following in their day-to-day actions:

- Build a history of competence and reliability. Finish what you start.

- Behave as if you are in business for yourself. Ask yourself, "If this were my ice cream store what would I do, what would I expect others to do?" You know, in reality, your career is your ice cream store!

- Don't just talk a good game, play a good game!

The 19th Hole

Wisdom and strength come from the courage to see things as they are.

Lao Tzu, ancient Chinese philosopher

Congratulations! You've played the full 18. Pour your favorite libation, sit down and put your feet up, it's time to reflect on your round.

The Global Leadership Course is a tough layout. The fairways are narrow, the rough is U.S. Open deep, and the pin settings on the greens are in difficult-to-reach positions. And, of course, sand, water, and trees do not make your shots any easier. But that's the game of leadership in today's world, a tough game to play.

As we mentioned back "On the Practice Tee," the intent of this book is to be helpful to you, the leader of people. I've tried not to be academic but to provide thoughts and suggestions that are useful and easily understood. In fact, I've tried to live up to the nickname given me by one of my high school teachers: "practical McHugh."

Golf is a metaphor for leadership. I hope you have come to agree with me. As a result, if you are a golfer, you may think more about your leadership as you play golf. Some of my caddies (critical helpers) in this effort have even said there are lessons in the book that will help them on the golf course! If you are a leader, and not a golfer, you may think more about golf as you lead and be a better leader for it. Many people are counting on you to play the game of leadership to the best of your ability. You can do it!

Hopefully, this book has provided some down-to-earth wisdom to help you play the tough holes as well as the easy ones.

We should take some time now to reflect on the 18 holes we've just played. You know, replay the holes on the videotape of our mind's eye. How did you score? What did you learn about your game? How have you been reinforced in your approach to the game? What do you need to do to be able to more effectively play the "leadership game?"

Serious golfers at this point will complete a "basic round chart," a typical format of which is shown in Figure 19-1.

As you can see, the chart covers the various elements of a round and the golfer records his or her performance on each hole. The golfer then reviews it and determines the areas of opportunity to improve and what might be done to achieve the desired improvement.

Over 100 years ago, James Braid, winner of five British Opens and designer of Gleneagles and many other famous Scottish golf courses, wrote in his *Golf Guide and How to Play Golf*:

> Golf [Leadership] is a game requiring an enormous amount of thought, and unless the player can always ascertain exactly what is the reason for his faults and what is the reason for his method of remedying them he will never make much progress. The more he thinks out the game for himself the better he will get on.[1]

Serious leaders should periodically prepare a "basic round chart" to assess how they are playing the game of leadership. You can make your own individualized chart. As an example, Figure 19-2 is a "basic leadership round chart" based on the selection of a key concept from each of the 18 holes of the Global Leadership Course that you just completed. Each hole is a par 4, for balance and ease of scoring. I suggest you assess your play on each hole and objectively score yourself. Scoring opportunities are par 4 (acceptable), birdie 3 (very good), eagle 2 (terrific), bogey 5 (close, but), and double bogey 6 (get help). Total your scores and measure the overall round against par 72.

FIGURE 19-1.
Golfer's basic round chart.

Hole	Fairway	Green	Putts	Up/Down	Sand Save	Pin High	Hazard	Penalty	Over/Under Par
1									
2									
3									
4									
5									
6									
7									
8									
9									
10									
11									
12									
13									
14									
15									
16									
17									
18									
Totals									

FIGURE 19-2.
Your basic leadership round chart.

Hole	(Comment)	Par	Score
1 Show passion and enthusiasm for what we do and share it with others.		4	
2 Keep the game of leadership as simple as I can.		4	
3 Make decisions based on my personal values and the core values of my organization.		4	
4 Follow leadership principles and rules based on morality and integrity.		4	
5 Demonstrate commitment to my organization's vision.		4	
6 Feel comfortable with my leadership grip (knowledge), stance (values), and swing (skills).		4	
7 Strive to be the best leader I can be.		4	
8 Focus on the situation, issue, or problem, not on the person.		4	
9 Accept responsibility for my actions.		4	
10 Demonstrate confidence in myself and in my people.		4	
11 Communicate performance goals, expectations, and measurements.		4	
12 Remain cool under fire.		4	
13 Recognize the positive contributions of others.		4	
14 Provide constructive feedback to my people.		4	
15 Accept change and adapt to it as encouragement to others.		4	
16 Provide help and support to others.		4	
17 Consistently exhibit positive and optimistic behavior.		4	
18 Know if it is to be, it is up to me.		4	
Total		72	

Comments: _____

_____

_____

Looking at your scorecard, you know you hit some good shots. You maintained a consistency of good play in several aspects of your leadership game. Let's have another "cool one" and toast the successes you are enjoying as a leader. You need to celebrate your accomplishments!

Now, as we continue to sip our refreshments, just as the serious golfer does, select your leadership areas that appear to need some work on the practice tee or putting green.

Probably the best place to begin will be to look at any bogies or double bogies scored on the course. If there are more than two or three, pick the ones you see as most important to work on. Once again, like the golfer, you don't want to start over with a new swing. See where you can make adjustments that will improve effectiveness. Develop your action plan for improving effectiveness, get the help you need, and put the plan into practice— "perfect practice"—as soon as you can. Golfers keep their "round charts" for reference and benchmarking. You can retain your leadership "round chart" as well and track your progress to increased leadership success. Remember, it's up to you.

Most golfers shoot scores higher than par for their rounds of golf. Yet, all golfers continuously aim to shoot what for each of them is the lowest achievable score. The effort at continuous improvement is never ending for every "real golfer," no matter how often and for how long they play the game. Golfers focus on the weaknesses in their game that, if improved, could lower their scores, such as driving distance, iron play, the short game, and putting. The quest is to add the fewest numbers to the blank scorecard over the 18 holes of play, knowing all the while that total perfection is not achievable.

The game of leadership is also a supreme test of a person's quest for perfection. Every leader, like the golfer, begins with a blank scorecard, that is, at 0 percent effectiveness. The goal for the "real leader" is to be 100 percent effective. It won't happen. But the "real leader" constantly works at continuous improvement, at being the most effective leader he or she can be. And as we have tried to point out, programs and touted panaceas won't do it for you. Your leadership greatness will come from within. As

Grantland Rice, the legendary sports writer, said in a 1920 edition of *American Golfer Magazine*, "Golf [leadership] is 20 percent mechanics and technique. The other 80 percent is philosophy, humor, tragedy, romance, melodrama, companionship, camaraderie, cussedness, and conversation."[2]

The golfer intent on improving his or her game takes away from each round the satisfaction of shots well made and holes well played. He or she also takes away a resolution to work on the improvement of two or three aspects of the game. Not a total overhaul but thoughts for tuning up their game. I hope you will look at what you have read in the same way. Congratulate yourself where you know you are playing well. Keep it up! Select two or three areas for improved effectiveness. Go to work on them! That's the way you can get better at the leadership game!

You can play golf for a long time provided you can still stand up and swing! You can play the leadership game even longer. It's a lifelong opportunity in careers, retirement, volunteerism, and always when it comes to setting a good example.

No mortal leader is perfect. You will make mistakes. But we all know we can play the leadership game more effectively. You can do a better job of helping others succeed. You can achieve the personal satisfaction of knowing you are making a valuable contribution to your organization and to the world in which we live. You will be playing the Global Leadership Course in par or better! Remember the holes and keep your ball in the fairway.

Golf and the Game of Leadership has allowed me the opportunity to share personal experiences and beliefs, practical tips and inspiring words from others, and my favorite stories about golf and leadership. I've enjoyed writing this book. I hope you enjoyed reading it.

Here's wishing you continuing great games of golf, leadership, and life!

The
Pro Shop

Notes

Hole #1

1. Randy Voorhees, *As Hogan Said . . . The 389 Best Things Ever Said About How to Play Golf* (New York: Simon & Schuster, 2000), p. 107.
2. Bob Kievra, "18 Million Ways to Say Thanks," Worcester, Massachusetts *Telegram & Gazette*, September 22, 2000. With permission.
3. Voorhees, *As Hogan Said*, p. 106.

Hole #2

1. Maryann Keller, *Rude Awakening, The Rise, Fall and Struggle for Recovery of General Motors* (New York: William Morrow and Company, 1989).
2. Ibid, pp. 238–239.
3. Bill Laimbeer, WJR Radio interview, *The Paul W. Smith Show*, October 29, 1997.
4. Troy Aikman, ABC-TV interview, *Regis and Kathy Lee Show*, August 22, 1997.

Hole #3

1. Michael Hiestand, "NBC's Miller Fills Void Left by Golf Stars," *USA Today*, March 7, 2003, p. 2C.
2. Noel M. Tichy, *The Leadership Engine* (New York: Harper Collins, 1997), p. 107.
3. General Electric Values. Reprinted with permission.

4. General Motors Values. Reprinted with permission.

5. Joan Magretta, *What Management Is: How It Works and Why It's Everyone's Business* (New York: Simon & Schuster, 2002), pp. 202–203.

Hole #4

1. Malcolm Campbell, *Ultimate Golf Techniques* (New York: DK Publishing Inc., 1996), p. 197.

2. Robin McMillan, *The Golfer's Home Companion* (New York: Simon & Schuster, 1993), p. 28.

3. The USGA, *2002–2003 Official Rules of Golf* (Chicago: Triumph Books, 2002), p.53.

4. Vince Flynn, *Term Limits* (New York: Pocket Books, 1999), p. 154.

5. "The Guy in the Glass," as written by Peter "Dale" Wimbrow, Sr. in 1934, and presented here with our thanks.

Hole #5

1. Joel Barker, *The Power of Vision* (Video). Charthouse Learning, 1991.

2. Deborah Graham, "Lose the First-Tee Jitters," *Senior Golfer*, June 1997, p. 92.

3. Viktor Frankl, *Man's Search for Meaning* (New York: Washington Square Press, 1963).

Hole #6

1. Dale Concannon, *Wise Words for Golfers* (New York: Thomas Dunne Books, 2000), p. 235.

2. Ibid, p.241.

3. Alex Taylor, III, "GM: Why They Might Break Up America's Biggest Company," *Fortune,* April 29, 1996, p. 84.

4. B.C. Forbes, "Editor's Comment," *Forbes,* October 7, 1996. Reprinted by permission of *Forbes* Magazine © 2003 Forbes, Inc.

5. Malcolm Campbell, *Ultimate Golf Techniques* (New York: DK Publishing Inc., 1996), p. 74.
6. Randy Voorhees, *As Hogan Said . . . The 389 Best Things Ever Said About How to Play Golf* (New York: Simon & Schuster, 2000), p. 104.

Hole #7

1. Doug Sanders, "My Shot," *Golf Digest,* August 2003, p. 114.

Hole #8

1. Tiger Woods (with the Editors of *Golf Digest*), *How I Play Golf* (New York: Warner Books, 2001), p. 85.

Hole #9

1. Christine Brennan, "Pure and Simple, Golf Should Be Put on Top of Sports Pedestal," *USA Today*, October 3, 2002, p. 3C.
2. Tamara Kaplan, "The Tylenol Crisis: How Effective Public Relations Saved Johnson & Johnson. Pennsylvania State University Web site: www.personal.psu.edu, 1998, p.3.

Hole #10

1. Tiger Woods (with the Editors of *Golf Digest*), *How I Play Golf* (New York: Warner Books, 2001), p. 257.
2. Bob Rotella, *Golf Is a Game of Confidence* (New York: Simon & Schuster, 1996).
3. John McCormick, "Even Tiger Needs a Trainer," *Newsweek,* December 9, 1996, p. 61.

Hole #11

1. Michael Bamberger, "A Woman Among Men," *Sports Illustrated,* February 24, 2003, p. 64.

2. Ron Shapiro and Mark Jankowski, *The Power of Nice* (New York: John Wiley & Sons, 1998).

3. Robert Browning, *A History of Golf* (London: JM Dent & Sons, 1955).

Hole #12

1. "World's Most Dangerous Golf Courses," *Men's Health*, April 1997.

2. Peggy Noonan, "Courage Under Fire," *Wall Street Journal*, October 5, 2001, editorial page.

3. Peter Koestenbaum, *Leadership: The Inner Side of Greatness* (San Francisco: Jossey-Bass, 1991), p. 92.

Hole #13

1. Bob Kievra, "18 Million Ways to Say Thanks," Worcester, Massachusetts *Telegram & Gazette*, September 18, 2000. With permission.

Hole #14

1. Bernard L. Rosenbaum, *How to Motivate Today's Worker* (New York: McGraw-Hill, 1982).

2. Edward J. Dwyer, "Seven Paradoxes of Leadership," *Journal for Quality and Participation*, March 1994.

Hole #16

1. Joel Barker, *The Power of Vision* (Video). Charthouse Learning, 1991.

Hole #17

1. Dennis N.T. Perkins, *Leading at the Edge* (New York: AMACOM, 2000), p. 40.

Hole #18

1. Bob Rotella, *Golf Is a Game of Confidence* (New York: Simon & Schuster, 1996), p. 237.

19th Hole

1. Dale Concannon, *Wise Words for Golfers* (New York: Thomas Dunne Books, 2000), p. 151.
2. Ibid, p. 90.

Glossary:
Golf Is a Way of Life with a Language All Its Own

Ace A hole in one.

Airmail the Green Ball flies over the green without touching it.

Amateur One who does not receive compensation for playing the game.

Back Nine The last nine holes of an 18-hole course.

Birdie A score of one under the par for a hole.

Bogey A score of one over the par for a hole.

Bunker A hazard filled with sand or grass that is placed where a fairway shot may end. You are not allowed to practice swing or ground your club in a bunker. Sand bunkers are commonly referred to as sand traps.

Caddie A person who carries a player's clubs and helps the player determine distances, club selection, and the line for putting.

Chip A low running shot played from near the edge of the green toward the hole.

Champions Tour Professional Golf Association (PGA) competitive tour for male golfers age 50 and over.

Course Rating The degree of difficulty of a course.

Cut The score at the end of 36 holes of a 72-hole tournament required to play the final 36 holes.

Divot Turf removed by the clubhead when a shot is played.

Dogleg A fairway that hooks to the left or right, obscuring the green from the tee.

Draw   A deliberate stroke for a right-handed player that causes the ball to curve from right to left in its flight. Opposite of a fade.

Drive   A shot from the tee area.

Driver   A golf club with a long shaft, large head, and little loft used for driving the ball for maximum distance off the tee.

Driving Range   Area set aside for practice.

Eagle   A score of two under the par for a hole.

Fade   A deliberate stroke for a right-handed player that causes the ball to curve from left to right in its flight. Opposite of a draw.

Fairway   The manicured playing area between the tee and the green that offers the player the best chance for success. Also known as "the short grass."

Feathery   Early type of golf ball made by filling a leather pouch with boiled feathers.

Front Nine   The first nine holes of an 18-hole course.

Green   The area of very short grass surrounding the hole where the player must use a putter to hit the ball.

Green in Regulation   The number of shots you are expected to play before getting your ball on the green. Always two shots less than par for the hole.

Guttie   This ball was introduced in 1848. It was made of gutta percha, a rubberlike substance from the latex of a Malaysian tree species. Less expensive than the feathery.

Hacker   A poor golfer.

Handicap   The average score of a player set against par.

Hazard   Permanent features of a golf course designed to obstruct play, such as sand traps, ponds, rivers, and trees.

Hole   General term for the area between tee and green. Also, the specific target on the green.

Hook   Unintentional stroke that causes the ball to bend sharply to the left for a right-handed player.

Interlocking Grip   To hold the club such that the little finger of one hand is wrapped around the forefinger of the other.

Lie   Position of the ball at rest.

Links   Golf course within four miles of the sea coast.

Loft   The angle of the clubface to the ground. Zero degree loft is perpendicular to the ground.

Lost Ball   Any ball that cannot be located once struck.

LPGA   Ladies Professional Golf Association.

Making the Cut   Qualifying for subsequent rounds in a tournament.

Match Play   Form of competition in which the number of holes won or lost by a player or team, rather than the number of strokes taken, determines the winner.

Medal Play   Form of competition in which the number of strokes a player takes to complete a round is compared with other players' scores for the round. Commonly called stroke play.

Mulligan   Allowing a player to replay any one shot on a hole without counting the shot replayed.

Nineteenth Hole   The clubhouse bar after playing 18 holes.

Par   Standard score for a hole based on the length of the hole and the number of strokes a very good player would expect to take to complete it in normal conditions.

Pin   Pole, with a flag attached, that marks the hole on each green.

Pitch   Lofted shot to the green with little run at the end of the ball's flight.

PGA   Professional Golf Association.

Professional   One who is compensated for playing the game.

Putt   Act of hitting the ball on the green with a putter.

Rough   Area of taller, unmown grass alongside the fairway, which punishes an off-line shot.

Round   18 holes of golf.

Rubber Core Ball   Revolutionized golf game at the turn of the twentieth century. Superseded the guttie. Modern balls are encased in either balata (soft) or surlyn (hard) covers. The balls differ in distance, spin, and durability.

Sandbagger   A hustler who maintains an artificially high handicap in order to win bets.

Scratch Golfer   A golfer whose handicap equals the par score of the golf course.

Short Game   Chipping, pitching, and putting.

Slice   Unintentional stroke that causes the ball to curve violently to the right for a right-handed player.

Tee   Closely mown area from which the first stroke on a hole is played. Also, a small peg on which the golf ball is placed.

Up and Down   An approach shot plus a single putt from anywhere off the green.

USGA   The United States Golf Association, golf's governing body in the USA and Mexico.

Vardon Trophy   Awarded annually to the professional golfer with the lowest scoring average on the PGA tour.

Whiff   Missing the ball during a swing.

Yips   To miss simple putts because of nerves.

Index